*The Continuing Witness
of the Missional Church*

The Continuing Witness of the Missional Church

Reflections on Darrell Guder's Life and Teaching

EDITED BY
JASON BYASSEE,
ALBERT Y. S. CHU,
TIM DICKAU,
ROSS A. LOCKHART,
AND ANDREA PERRETT

CASCADE *Books* · Eugene, Oregon

THE CONTINUING WITNESS OF THE MISSIONAL CHURCH
Reflections on Darrell Guder's Life and Teaching

Copyright © 2025 Wipf and Stock Publishers. All rights reserved. Except for brief quotations in critical publications or reviews, no part of this book may be reproduced in any manner without prior written permission from the publisher. Write: Permissions, Wipf and Stock Publishers, 199 W. 8th Ave., Suite 3, Eugene, OR 97401.

Cascade Books
An Imprint of Wipf and Stock Publishers
199 W. 8th Ave., Suite 3
Eugene, OR 97401

www.wipfandstock.com

PAPERBACK ISBN: 979-8-3852-3825-5
HARDCOVER ISBN: 979-8-3852-3826-2
EBOOK ISBN: 979-8-3852-3827-9

Cataloguing-in-Publication data:

Names: Byassee, Jason, editor. | Chu, Albert Y. S., editor. | Dickau, Tim, editor. | Lockhart, Ross A., editor. | Perrett, Andrea, editor.

Title: The continuing witness of the missional church : reflections on Darrell Guder's life and teaching / edited by Jason Byassee, Albert Y. S. Chu, Tim Dickau, Ross A. Lockhart, and Andrea Perrett.

Description: Eugene, OR : Cascade Books, 2025 | Includes bibliographical references.

Identifiers: ISBN 979-8-3852-3825-5 (paperback) | ISBN 979-8-3852-3826-2 (hardcover) | ISBN 979-8-3852-3827-9 (ebook)

Subjects: LCSH: Guder, Darrell L., 1939–. | Mission of the church. | Church. | Evangelistic work. | Missions.

Classification: BV601.8. C66 2025 (paperback) | BV601.8. C66 (ebook)

06/06/25

Unless otherwise noted, Scripture quotations are taken from the Holy Bible, New Revised Standard Version (NRSV) Bible, copyright 1989, Division of Christian Education of the National Council of the Churches of Christ in the United States of America. Used by permission. All rights reserved.

Scripture quotations marked (NIV) are taken from the Holy Bible, New International Version®, NIV®. Copyright © 1973, 1978, 1984, 2011 by Biblica, Inc.™ Used by permission of Zondervan. All rights reserved worldwide. www.zondervan.com The "NIV" and "New International Version" are trademarks registered in the United States Patent and Trademark Office by Biblica, Inc.™

Scripture quotations marked THE MESSAGE Copyright © by Eugene H. Peterson 1993, 1994, 1995, 1996, 2000, 2001, 2002. Used by permission of Tyndale House Publishers, Inc.

Scripture quotations marked (ESV) are taken from The Holy Bible, English Standard Version® Text Edition: 2016. Copyright © 2001 by Crossway, a publishing ministry of Good News Publishers. The ESV® text has been reproduced in cooperation with and by permission of Good News Publishers. Unauthorized reproduction of this publication is prohibited. All rights reserved.

For Darrell and Judy Guder,
whose vision, encouragement, and prayerful support
helped created and catalyze
the Centre for Missional Leadership's ministry.

Contents

Introduction ix

Missional Theology Shaping the Church and World

1 Darrell's Worthy Walk 3
  Jason Byassee

2 Co-Workers in the Gospel: How Being Apprenticed
  to Darrell Guder Transformed My Ministry 12
  Ross A. Lockhart

3 Speak Softly and Carry a Pencil: Glimpses of Walking Worthily 21
  Sarah Bixler

4 Creational Theology Is Missional Theology 30
  Jonathan R. Wilson

5 A Unique Partnership: Young Life and the Lutheran Church
  of Württemberg 40
  Christoph Schneider

6 Para-Church Ministries: Parasites or Partners? 47
  David J. Montgomery

Missional Theology Shaping Specific Communities

7 Living the Missional Call 59
  Thomas Daniel

8 For the Beauty of Chestermere: Darrell Guder and the Proximal
  Imagination 65
  Preston Pouteaux

9	Tents and Tabernacles *Albert Y. S. Chu*	71
10	The Missional Garden in a Pluralist City *Konnie Vissers*	78
11	"You Are My Witnesses": Now and New *Renée and James B Notkin*	85

Missional Theology Shaping Discipleship

12	Lessons from a Theological Hero *Keas Keasler*	95
13	Shepherding into the Sending Flow of God's Love: Gospel-Centric Relational Witness in the Congregation *Kurt Helmcke*	101
14	The Gospel We Live *Doug Kelly*	110
15	A Fitting Benediction: Darrell Guder, Teacher, Pastor, and Visionary *Chris Currie*	119
16	The Continuing Conversion of the Church in Our Cultural Moment *Tim Dickau*	127

Missional Theology Shaping Vocation

17	When I Preach, I Preach Darrell Guder *Andrea Perrett*	139
18	A Challenge to the Entire Body of Christ *David Jennings*	148
19	A Vision for the Praying Church *Grant Vissers*	156
20	Darrell Who? *Corey Schlosser-Hall*	165
21	Through the Roof Medicine *Toby Long*	172
	Afterword *Mark Glanville*	183
	Contributors	189
	Bibliography	193

Introduction

THIS BOOK IS A carefully crafted and curated collection of essays in honor of the influential missiologist Dr. Darrell Guder. Darrell is a renowned thought leader in the missional church movement, knowing for helping the global church reflect theologically on its witness as Christians move more fully into a post-Christendom era. For over six decades, Darrell's impact in church and academia have been far reaching across Christian traditions with profound impact across North America and around the world.

An early participant in the Gospel and Our Culture Network, Darrell helped in the research and writing that produced the seminal text, *Missional Church*, for which he is the named editor. Darrell is known to countless students as a beloved professor, with posts at several colleges including Whitworth University, Louisville Presbyterian Theological Seminary, Columbia Theological Seminary, and Princeton Theological Seminary. To others he is known as a prolific translator of Karl Barth, a thought leader with para-church ministries in the United States and Europe, and a well-respected participant in the global theological discourse, where he is recognized as a senior scholar fiercely committed to ecumenism and the unity of the church. However, Darrell is not only known for his academic achievements and professional posts, but he is also known for the depth of his character and the quality of the relationships fostered over the years. Darrell is treasured as a mentor, colleague, advisor, and friend.

This collection of essays attempts to capture and honor who Darrell is, what he has done, and more importantly *the impact and influence* on others through his faithful witness to the gospel of Jesus Christ. The authors of this book explore how Darrell's life and teaching have impacted the church and its witness and how Darrell's thought continues to shape the missional conversation today. The aim is not only to talk about his past impact, but also to articulate how Darrell's vision can continue to point toward the vital ways in which followers of Christ are called to bear witness to the healing of the nations in our time and place. This is a hopeful action, and one that will not leave the church unchanged, but rather will transform it so that the posture of the Christian community toward culture is not hostile, but open instead—possessing a joy that comes with being Christian. This collection of essays is offered in gratitude to God and as a humble tribute to the life and work of Darrell Guder; however, we acknowledge gratefully that there is already a wonderful Festschrift published in Darrell's honor entitled *Converting Witness*. That work celebrated his theological contribution and was primarily directed toward an academic audience. This project seeks a different audience. Here, we still honor Darrell's theological contribution to the life of the mind; however, we also seek to shine a light on Guder's ongoing impact upon the church and its mission in the world.[1]

Darrell has influenced, mentored, and formed a multitude of students over the years, both through his teaching and his books. Furthermore, some people have been shaped not only by Darrell's words but also by the way in which he has lived his life in service to the gospel. You will note how many of our authors also praise Darrell's wife Judy in sharing and showing the gospel through her scholarship, hospitality, and love of music. It is not an understatement to say that Darrell has shaped a generation of missional leaders now leading the church across North America and around the world. As Darrell approached his eighty-fifth birthday in November 2024, the editors of this book from the Centre for Missional Leadership (CML) in Vancouver set out to capture a sense of how Darrell as a person and as a theologian has impacted the church and changed lives for good. Therefore, this collection of essays offers a few of the stories of those living out their missional vocation through the

---

1 In the Centre for Missional Leadership at St. Andrew's Hall, we focus on equipping leaders (lay and clergy) for their witness in the world. Therefore, it is important to note that one does not need a graduate theological education to understand and appreciate this book. While many of the main tenets of missional theology are summarized in the essays that follow, if you need a primer or refresher on the topic, we shamelessly recommend Darrell's book *Called to Witness*.

church, university, law, medicine, and more, who have been profoundly blessed and significantly shaped by Darrell Guder's life and witness.

The Vision for This Book

Now if you know Darrell through his broad-reaching academic contributions you might be wondering why a missional leadership center at a Presbyterian theological college in Vancouver, Canada, would edit a book like this to honor him. Simply put, we have been deeply marked and transformed by Darrell's wisdom, kindness, and friendship, and therefore seek to celebrate him (and Judy), with a strong desire to share his impact with a wider audience. CML at St. Andrew's Hall is an education and equipping ministry for the wider, ecumenical church across North America that has been shaped by Darrell Guder in his retirement years. At an individual level, the leadership team at the CML are part of the generation whose scholarship and discipleship have been directly impacted by Darrell's life and witness. At an institutional level, the CML itself bears witness to Darrell's vision of missional thinking and has been carefully built over time with his direct input and guidance. Since the CML was created ten years ago, under the leadership of Rev. Dr. Ross Lockhart, Darrell has been an integral part of our community serving as the senior fellow in residence. In his mentorship of CML, Darrell has inspired and enlivened our work, speaking across Canada and the Pacific Northwest, helping to shape programs of the CML, as well as guiding and endorsing several publications. Darrell's impact and missional fingerprints are all over our organization and our lives. We are so deeply honored that Darrell has given so much to us in this season of his life after retirement from full-time teaching, and this book is a small way of saying thank you.

We know our story is only one of many. Not only has Darrell made big splashes with his impact on institutions, communities, and individuals, but also the ripples of his life continue to spread throughout the world, influencing countless lives and communities. We hope that this collection of essays honors his ongoing impact.

The Design of This Book

The essays in this book sketch a portrait of someone who has lived their life in a way that embodies incarnational witness. What follows in the pages ahead is not a complete rendering of Darrell; this only scratches the surface of who this beloved child of God is in our shared experience. However, these stories and reflections sketch an imprint of a faithful disciple who has endeavored to walk worthily, to do theology humbly, and to be an incarnational witness, all in service of the gospel.

One of the joys of this project was reflecting on the diverse and eclectic ways in which Darrell has influenced so many of us through his life and witness. Some of the essays capture how Darrell has impacted the theological discourse, shape, and witness of the broader church, while other writers detail how a leader's own approach to ministry in general has been transformed. Several essays document how specific witnessing communities have been directly shaped by Darrell's influence, yet other essays address specific aspects of vocation which he has helped develop through his writing and personal interactions.

As you read the stories about Darrell's influence on theology, the church, ministries, communities, and vocations, we invite you to notice some of the recurring themes and situations. The oft-repeated stories of Darrell inviting people into his home or embarking on years-long discipleship journey with a student provide a tangible, enfleshed depiction of Darrell's life and witness. This is a rare quality to have such a deep integration of one's faith and theology. It can be difficult to separate his theological influence from the influence of his person, which speaks to how Darrell has lived his life as an incarnational witness.

As you approach these essays, we offer three lenses to aid you in observing this impact, using concepts drawn directly from Darrell's own work: how individuals have been shaped into *witnesses*, how they have been equipped in *equipping the saints*, and how they have learned to *walk worthily*. Not surprisingly, you will also note that the authors themselves frequently draw on these lenses to help describe Darrell's influence.

We invite you to notice how leaders and their communities have become *witnesses* to the gospel. These essays are a sampling of how leaders have incarnationally responded to the question often posed by Darrell, "How then shall we witness?" Through Darrell's influence, either briefly or over the span of decades, these leaders describe how they have leaned into the missional call to be a witness themselves, how they have stayed faithful to the call to be witnesses and have painted a picture of their own context, as if to say, "this is how we have witnessed."

Perhaps *equipping the saints* is a more helpful lens for you to consider Darrell's influence. Some of the following essays demonstrate how leaders and communities have been equipped to equip the saints. Through his own life and witness, Darrell has contributed to building up the body of Christ by equipping a multitude of leaders for service. This equipping by Darrell of missional leaders has led to further equipping by those saved to be sent, in a way that only the Holy Spirit can orchestrate. Indeed, the stories that you will encounter in this book express often how leaders have been more effectively equipped by Darrell and his teaching in order to build up others in mature Christian faith, so that they, in turn, can further extend the equipping of others for the service of the gospel.[2]

While there are surely other lenses to consider Darrell's influence on the church and academy, for the purposes of this book we invite you to notice one last lens, *walking worthily*. What follows in this book are stories of Christians whose pilgrimage with God, from baptism to life's end, bear testimony to the mentorship of Darrell that has helped them to grow into their vocation of "walking worthily." As Darrell once wrote, "As the missional leadership of the community walks worthy of its calling, it equips the entire community of saints to do so."[3] The stories of these leaders are a testament to how they have been challenged, encouraged, and (re)formed by Darrell to live up to the calling of Christ in Scripture to "walk worthily."

Joining the Missional Conversation

We acknowledge that the authors included in this publication are just a small sample of those who have been influenced by Darrell's life and witness. We recognize that most of the contributors are either connected to Darrell through his time at Princeton, or through the geographic proximity of the Pacific Northwest. We also know that there is likely more of a Canadian perspective than most would expect in a book written about an American theologian (but we won't apologize for that!).

Perhaps you, the reader, have your own story to add. Perhaps you know Darrell personally and have a story like Konnie, Corey, or Chris that begins with, "I remember the first time I met Darrell Guder . . ." Or perhaps you were a student, like Kurt, Doug, or Thomas who were invited into Darrell's home and graciously welcomed not only by him, but also by his wife Judy. Maybe you are someone who has primarily been influenced

---

2. Guder, *Called to Witness*, 145.
3. Guder, *Called to Witness*, 155.

and impacted, formed and shaped, through second- or third-degree connections with Darrell, like David, Christoph or Preston. Or perhaps you have noticed Darrell's words and wisdom surfacing in your writing, preaching, prayer, or actions, like Andrea, Grant, or Sarah.

Regardless of your connection or story, if you are reading this book you are a participant in the ongoing and expanding missional conversion of the church of which the CML seeks to foster from our diverse, secular, and post-Christendom West Coast setting. While reading the essays in the chapters ahead, we invite you to fill in the gaps of this sketch of Darrell, noting the impact on *your own* life, ministry, and witness. At the end of each essay, we have included some reflection questions. These can be answered as an individual or in a group discussion, and you do not have to know Darrell personally to engage with these reflection questions.

Now, perhaps the authors in the book gush a bit too much in our gratitude for Darrell. While we know that there are other people who have influenced our ministry, this collection gathers the influence from Darrell in one place. We are bold to claim that the influence of Darrell Guder's life and teaching *on our lives* has helped formed us into better witnesses of the gospel. We don't share these stories for the sake of highlighting our own sanctification, nor do we do so to build up Darrell (something he would not like at all!), but rather we share them because of what they *reveal* about the gospel, and how they can educate, edify, and equip the saints to bear further witness to God's reconciling love for the world made know in the risen and returning Lord Jesus.

Locating This Work in the Wider Missional Theology Conversation

You will note when reading each chapter that the authors reflect a certain position within the missional theology conversation. It should come as no surprise that the CML's location within the discourse aligns with Darrell's core tenets of missional theology, given his foundational role and ongoing influence in our college. While we recognize that there is diversity in theology and opinion among the authors, overall, they have been curated to affirm the distinctiveness of Darrell's missional theology. While "missional" language might be a bit overused and perhaps even falling out of fashion, these essays are a testament that leaders, communities, and institutions have seen great fruit in the incarnational witness of the gospel.

In particular, we wish to highlight a few aspects about what we value regarding Darrell's ongoing contribution to the missional theology conversation. The first facet we treasure is his rich integration of theological discourse and practice. This position stands out in a culture where there has been a tendency to go straight to the pragmatic and sideline the theological framing with the consultant's expediency and a default to "tips and tricks theology." Being "missional" can be too easily commodified, but for Darrell, there is no normative form of the missional church.[4] His work has not been about finding the right technique or identifying a model to replicate; rather he has focused on missional engagement that balances a community's gifts with a strong dose of dependence upon the Holy Spirit. For Darrell, one cannot have theological discourse without considering and integrating how a community lives out its witness to a waiting, watching world. Throughout his career Darrell has not been content to keep theology cordoned off in the academy but has consistently integrated theology into his own practice in a way that moved the church toward deep, reflective thinking amid holistic transformative action. Thus, the visible, tangible, concrete experiences of missional communities, as formed by the Holy Spirit, are to be witnesses to Jesus Christ as integral to theological discourse.

A second feature of Darrell's distinctiveness that we wish to highlight is the way in which he has approached his theological contributions with a light-handedness and without a need to control the outcome. Throughout his career he has graciously provided his contribution to theological discourse, then allowed it to be received and take root in other arenas beyond his control. Darrell has often mentioned his genuine surprise that *Missional Church*, so clearly meant for a North American audience, has taken on a life of its own around the world in such divergent places as Europe, South Korea, and South Africa. Darrell consistently takes the risk of offering what he can, while encouraging others to pick up and continue the discourse from their own vantage point. This light-handedness is important, especially considering that much has changed since the 1990s when missional church conversation was almost exclusively inhabited by white, Western, male scholars and pastors. As the conversation is slowly moving beyond these confines, Darrell's theological contributions have

---

4. Guder, *Continuing Conversion of the Church*, 147.

been humbly offered up for other voices to extend the conversation in their own context. Darrell is someone who, even in his ninth decade of life, responds with glee and delight in how others have taken up and extended the missional conversation and become participants in the process of the missional conversion of the church.

This brings us to the last aspect we wish to highlight regarding Darrell's distinctiveness in the missional church conversation: humility. We noted previously Darrell's encouragement of others to take up the mantel of the missional church discussion without claiming proprietary rights, but Darrell's humility is more than his desire to see others "in the spotlight." Now, Darrell would never be one to recognize this in himself (to do so would negate the characteristic); however, nearly forty years ago he wrote about doing modest theology, where the humility of the gospel would be reflected in the way that we do theology together as a Christian community. He put a call out for an "incarnational" way of doing theology, where theology would be dynamic and modest, grow and mature. Darrell desired that incarnational theology would be careful to avoid arrogantly superior and exclusive definitions and prescriptions of a North American centric worldview, and instead be open to enormous diversity of expression and thought. Darrell thought that incarnational theology would encourage alternate ways of attending to God's Holy Spirit at work in the church and the world while being alert to our own cultural bondage as North Americans in a late-stage capitalistic context and the reductionistic limits of our own cultural bondage. Darrell looked forward to being surprised by the future tense of our faith.[5] In this publication, as we reflect on Darrell's influence on theology and practice, we affirm that he has indeed lived theologically in a way that reflects the humility of the gospel. Furthermore, this incarnational theology is reflected in the humble and faithful way in which he has lived his life with Judy. As the essays that follow attest, Darrell has lived into his calling of vocational witness both in the academy and in his personal life of discipleship. He has lived a life that is worthy of the calling of Christ.

As you continue, we trust that you will see our intention to honor Darrell as a scholar, pastor, and person of deep and humble Christian faith while also bearing witness in our own fragile and fallible human lives to the saving presence, power, and purpose of the triune God. We do so, trusting that the divine intentionality of the Holy Spirit has enabled

---

5. Guder, *Be My Witnesses*, 89–90.

the witness of the gospel to take root in each of the different contexts present in this book. Therefore, wherever you read this work, we trust also that *your* life, and that of your community, can also be a witness to the love of God who is at work in the world reconciling all of creation for the sake of the healing of the nations.

Missional Theology Shaping the Church and World

1

Darrell's Worthy Walk

Jason Byassee

When he was nine or ten years old, a little boy in Southern California read a missionary biography that inspired him. He too would become a missionary in the South Pacific. He even had the specific island picked out where he wanted to go. That was how we thought about mission in those days. You went somewhere exotic, dangerous, brave, and exciting. You told the people there about Jesus so that they, like we, might be saved. Countless Christian kids in Europe and North America had thought about missions that way since the birth of the modern missionary movement in the early nineteenth century. Catholic kids had done so as well for even longer, back to the sixteenth century.

Lots of us grow up from our dreams of becoming a professional athlete, an astronaut, a pop star, a firefighter. Most of our dreams are much too big. Young Darrell Guder's problem was that his dream was much too small. In time, he would end up lecturing in Asia and the South Pacific, but he did so much more. Darrell helped change the way all of us think about missions, from the white person traveling somewhere exotic, to mission being the entire purpose for every church's existence. God does not send lonely, heroic individuals. God sends the whole church. The church exists to be a people whose sending bears witness to the resurrection. Whether in the ruins of the church in decayed Christendom, or in the flush of new life of churches in Africa or Asia or Latin America, all Christians are missionaries now. And the "prize" of saving individual souls is much too small. The entire church is slowly starting to realize that our very existence is mission*al*, thanks in no small part to that young boy in Southern California.

It is not surprising that Darrell had such dreams from a young age. He describes his parents as serious and well-read lay theologians, discussing matters of faith and real life every time they gathered at the dinner table. Such conversations were "realistic and not hyper-pious." His parents cursed. They also prayed. When they faced the troubles we all do, like disease or job loss or moving, God was an agent in those stories. From his elementary school days "being a follower of Jesus was just what it meant to be alive," Darrell said. Looking back now, as a retiree up the West Coast from SoCal in the Seattle area, Darrell pauses when reflecting on his childhood: "I've been in Christian education since . . . as long as I can remember."

Evangelicals are famous for our emphasis on the dramatic, one-time conversion. St. Paul on the road to Damascus captures our imagination—some would say warps it. We lose Paul's praise of the mother and grandmother of his protégé Timothy, from whom he inherited the faith as they prayed and cursed together (2 Tim 1:5). Guder's entry into faith was more of the latter sort. But make no mistake: his was an evangelical upbringing. His parents threw in with the powerhouse First Presbyterian Church of Hollywood, where no less a luminary than Miss Henrietta Mears held court in Sunday School for decades. Her "class" numbered more than six thousand pupils at one point. This firebrand in mid-century evangelicalism had an even greater impact through her one-on-one mentorship of the future founders of Young Life, World Vision, and Campus Crusade for Christ, alongside no less than Billy Graham himself. Her winsome and personable evangelicalism infused their organizations with that movement's best instincts: blessing the world, loving the neighbor, and investing in other people via one-on-one mentoring. To see her legacy, you need to look no further than the string of vibrant Presbyterian churches that still wreath the West Coast of North America. For Mears had the wherewithal to send students to Princeton Theological Seminary rather than, say, more fundamentalist options.

Miss Mears may have had no seminary degree, let alone a doctorate, though esteemed institutions like Wheaton and Fuller begged her to come teach for them all the same (in evangelical land, "impact" trumps credentials every time). What she had was a genius's eye for observing young people and youth culture, one carried over into the institutions she indirectly helped found. For example, she had a habit of noticing the key leader in a group of young people and nurturing that one toward faith so that he would "pied-piper" all his friends along with him. Go meet with the student body president at USC, or the quarterback at UCLA, lead that one to Jesus, and watch as all his fans flock to Hollywood Pres and a life of ministry. This came to be called the "key kid" concept—the notion that evangelism works from the top-down. It remains controversial, not because it doesn't work, but because it sits ill with Jesus' own practice and teachings.

Darrell Guder was not, himself, a key kid in the way Miss Mears meant. Asked about his connection to the grande dame of evangelicalism, Darrell demurs. "I was never one of her 'boys.'" All the same, she made Hollywood Pres a powerhouse for Christian families, encouraging countless parents, like Darrell's, to the sorts of intentional conversations about faith that make for mature disciples. One need not visit the South Pacific to be a missionary, one only needs to make breakfast and take the kids to school.

Here's how much of a not-key kid Darrell was. He was neither a campus celebrity nor a quarterback. He was in the marching band at UCLA. His instrument was . . . wait for it . . . the glockenspiel. Darrell describes practicing elaborately to perform "Everything's Up to Date in Kansas City" at halftime of a football game at the L.A. Coliseum. He knew he was to march in a straight line toward a skyscraper that loomed over the top of the arena. "I made a flamboyant turn and marched toward the center of the field—all alone and about ten measures early," he remembers. Somehow over the din he heard the conductor shout, "Guder! Get the hell back here!" So he made another flamboyant turn and marched back to the sideline, still hammering on that German instrument.

Some march to the beat of their own . . . glockenspiel. What's the cliché in the leadership literature? If you think you're leading an institution and you turn around and no one is following, then you're not leading at all—you're just out for a walk.

It will surprise no one to learn that Darrell was an excellent student, flying through UCLA and planning to study abroad to learn the German language necessary to become a proper theologian. He had always been aware of the Swiss provenance of his surname and had traveled to Switzerland when he was seventeen to meet and get to know distant relatives, who quickly became friends. Once he arrived in Germany as an exchange student, he quickly became bilingual, and even more quickly acculturated. "I fit in there like a hand in a glove. I felt completely at home culturally." He never went back to UCLA, finished his university work in Germany with a PhD, without a seminary degree. Darrell has joked in public that he didn't figure out what he wanted to do with his life until he was fifty-one years old: a joke that plays well with confused fellow seminary students and graduates (that is, pretty much all of us). Only at fifty-one did he realize he had always been a missiologist committed to Christian education. But he never lacked for direction in his studies. "I didn't seek any of this out, it came to me," he said, with German faculty mentors and friends encouraging him to stay and study. The Los Angeles Presbytery ended up ordaining him to a Lutheran ministry in Germany, with neither party exactly sure whether what they were doing was proper polity-wise, but both sure it had never been done before and never would be again. Darrell's *sui generis* genius has long been to pull parties together who would naturally be foreign or suspicious to one another, but who once together feel like they've always trusted one another.

His first ministry in Germany was one every mainline church would wish to be able to hire for. The recent confirmands in a Hamburg suburb seemed to take their confirmation as a graduation ceremony right out of the church. Darrell was hired to go get them and reengage them with church life. He was not much older than they. He was, however, quite different culturally, as an evangelical from SoCal. But he spoke their language, both as a fluent German-speaker and a quick-study student of culture. Darrell found his charges "bright, open, and engageable," on their way to further study in German Gymnasien (academically inclined high schools) and universities. He was also in a perfect position to practice what he'd imbibed, by osmosis, via Henrietta Mears. Go to where the students are. Don't preach at them or embarrass them—they have parents and teachers for that. No, just love them where they are. Listen to them. Learn from them. And when they love and trust you enough to ask for help on the big-ticket questions in life, open up about your love for and trust in Jesus Christ. Young Lifers rhapsodize about "earning the right to be heard." Darrell was the perfect pioneer for this sort of ministry, not only for his theological and ministerial instincts, but because of his PhD work: he wouldn't even have been admitted to the Gymnasien without it. "It was all very strategic, but I had never thought about it before. I was called to outreach ministry, and it was all enabled by my university identity." Miss Mears: you may need to rethink your notion of what makes for a "key kid." Young Life is still going strong in Germany, as you will read in this book, pioneered by an American future missiologist.

Some in Darrell's evangelical orbit have always been suspicious of the possible "liberal" influence of his German education. But, of course, all North Americans like the prestige of European universities, if the American student can keep their head down and survive the piety-disdaining inquisitors. Darrell found there instead friends and encouragement and fresh ministry challenges. Then, degree in hand, Darrell organized a five-month speaking and preaching tour for one of his most renowned teachers, Professor Helmut Thielicke, whose sermons and essays were being read with sympathy by American evangelicals. He had, however, been critical of Billy Graham's revivals. A postwar crusade in Hamburg had seemed to Thielicke the height of American cultural insensitivity and historical know-nothingism. Raucous and emotional crowds did not play in post-Hitler Germany. When Graham heard that Thielicke was in Southern California, preaching in Hollywood Pres's orbit, he invited his critic to a crusade as a platform guest. Thielicke was more "curious than critical," so off he and Darrell went, back to the L.A. Coliseum, as it happens. Thielicke was greeted like a foreign dignitary or head of state, vetted by security, and marched to the platform, where Darrell translated Graham's brief sermon in whispered German. As folks streamed forward in response to Graham's invitation, Thielicke looked around for what he expected would be triumphalistic expressions on the faces of crusade staff. Instead, Thielicke said, "I couldn't see them because they were all praying." Thielicke changed his mind somewhat about Graham's work. In a later-published letter, Graham agreed that his work was inadequate in many ways, but what was he to do when the church so badly neglected the task of evangelism? Thielicke learned from Graham that preaching must always lead to invitation, because that's what the gospel does.

If you'll forgive the whiplash from one coast to another, from one theological tradition to its near-opposite: Thielicke had an invitation to preach to Harvard's Memorial Chapel in November 1963, which turned out to be the Sunday after John F. Kennedy's assassination. He phoned his hosts to beg off the assignment, since surely there would be someone else better situated to speak to so American a tragedy. The answer came back, "Professor Thielicke, there is nobody here who knows what to say either. Would you please come and speak to us?" Both Thielicke's correspondence with Graham and the Harvard sermon were subsequently published and widely read and engaged.[1] Sometimes you march out in front with your glockenspiel and . . . everybody follows.

Darrell has been married to Judy for forty-four years now—long enough that one might not stop to do the math and realize that they are a second marriage for each. A divorced theologian might not be a problem at Harvard or Princeton, but a divorce could still cost someone a job in evangelicalism today. Fifty years ago, it could in the Presbyterian church—which in those days formally reassessed a divorcé's ministry. Darrell welcomed the process, since he himself wondered whether his divorce rendered his ministry questionable. Darrell still calls his divorce "the worst thing that ever happened to me." For Darrell, "the fact that I met and married Judy was what saved my life." She was, and is, God's instrument of healing for him. Judy took a bit more convincing: "I wasn't very impressed with him when we first met!" she said. She got to know him better through hearing him teach a Bible study, appreciating his broadly evangelical posture: "too liberal for the conservatives and too conservative for the liberals." The Guders have formed a partnership as translators of significant theological texts from German. Surprisingly, Judy had no previous German-language expertise. She had been a French major and dreamed about living there. Studying German and living there instead turned out to be "not a chore, but fun." They also took part together in raising Judy's three sons and Darrell's son and daughter.

Judy tells a story about her time dating Darrell. He was then, as often since, committed to wearing a clerical collar. It was a way of marking himself off as a churchman within a culture like Young Life where the church was often suspect. He wore the collar all the time, including when he would go out on dates with Judy. Darrell was fascinated at the people who would approach him, total strangers who would divulge and want to discuss their problems. While appreciative, Judy suggested he shelve the collar for their dates. "Maybe it's time to take that off," she suggested. "It looks like you're a Catholic priest dating a parishioner!"

One of Darrell's protégés, Craig Barnes, later became president of Princeton Theological Seminary (PTS). He tells a story of the Guders' lavish hospitality that illustrates the fruit born of their marriage, not just

---

1. See Thielicke, *Notes from a Wayfarer*.

as parents and translators, but as missional people themselves. The Guders would regularly host a large Christmas party, inviting over friends from both the seminary and from Nassau Presbyterian Church. The centerpiece for the party would be a Swiss cheese of which Darrell was very proud. Called raclette, it requires a special grill they had purchased in Switzerland. Actually, they had purchased several of them, and folks would line up in rows as Darrell opined about its virtues. Barnes said, "I didn't care for this stinky smelly stuff at all. It was horrible. It should come with a disclaimer and a clothes pin for your nose." But Barnes was impressed with the ensemble of people. Lots of parties in academic towns see faculty come over with spouses, maybe a few students. But the Guders' house would be full of folks not involved with the seminary who lived nearby, or others who'd never heard of PTS but were leaders in the community, or in other religious traditions, or some friend from another part of the globe who happened to be staying with the Guders. "Darrell's idea of a great party is people who don't know each other well who get to know one another." Jack Fortin even finds a note of Guder's deep-seated Presbyterianism in the raclette parties. Fondue is messy; it gets everywhere. But good Swiss raclette is always done "decently and in good order."

Lots of people graduate out of evangelicalism. Darrell has frequently commented that this important term has become virtually unusable because of its being coopted politically. Academia is one common escape route. But Darrell never left, let alone did he go around telling disparaging stories about it. He went to work for Young Life to help train their staff in the treasury of wisdom of the church. As the story about Graham above illustrates, evangelical ministries often arise out of frustration with the broader, more liberal church shirking its duties. This can naturally lend to a kind of triumphalism in the para-church organization, thinking it does best the thing that Jesus most prizes. Darrell was having none of it. He would wear his clerical collar not just out on dates, but into the office at Young Life. Others might be in jeans and sweats, trying to relate to teenagers dressed the same way. Darrell looked like a German theologian. He would talk about unknown concepts like "the lectionary." And he would take on shibboleths most would avoid. "Para-church is a dreadful term," he said. "It ends up meaning 'not-quite-church,' which is not the way the New Testament understands the character of called communities." Darrell experimented with the Catholic language of "orders" as a more appropriate category for Young Life's evangelistic work among young people. He also introduced Young Life to a dozen or more seminaries willing to work with them, seeding relationships that continue to this day. He also met Young Lifers who had grown uncomfortable with the key-kid concept, or the inflexible five talks staffers are supposed to give. Darrell could show them the gospel has deeper resources, even if portions of evangelicalism were then unaware.

The challenge of those years was not unidirectional. Jack Fortin suggests Young Life did something for Darrell as well. Darrell had flown through his student years, so he "never really got into university life." Young Life became that for Darrell. "He was delightful. His beauty was he was able to laugh a bit about himself—because he was just so not-Young-Life. And he brought great humour with him." Fortin recounts Darrell enacting a then-famous comedy sketch from "Beyond the Fringe," in which an unbearably pompous English vicar gives a sermon on the verse from Genesis, "And Esau was a hairy man." Darrell memorized it and delivered it often. Not only that—he translated into German and managed to make even grim fellow Teutonics laugh at the skit. Darrell's dexterity with translation pushes into surprising new frontiers.

When he wasn't doing comedy written by Brits for Americans translated into German, Darrell was learning to be an administrator. Perhaps he was born to be one. Barnes was president of PTS after Darrell had been its dean and remembers how many procedures he followed had been hammered out meticulously by Darrell. "Administration is easy for him," Fortin observes. "He can do it in his sleep. Then he doesn't get consumed by it all day." Barnes remembers how well-organized Darrell is, which is part of the secret for his voluminous publishing productivity, in addition to stints in administration at Whitworth College and PTS. The myth of the absent-minded professor finds no purchase in Darrell's life—he can organize whole institutions' lives, not just his own.

This biographical essay could continue deeper into Darrell's academic career and theological contributions. But other essays in this volume will cover those topics. I'd like to leave you instead with a glimpse of Darrell's ministry in his retirement. Judy tells on Darrell: he has been offering a Bible study for their neighbors in their Seattle community. Attendees come not because of his accolades or plaudits. They come because he loves teaching Scripture, and everybody loves learning from someone who loves what they are teaching. "His Bible study is really well received here," Judy told me. "People really enjoy it. He gets about fifteen of them." As the missional church has taught the rest of us—all the risen Christ does is raise up communities that bear witness to himself.

For Reflection

1. If Darrell is right, and mission is something the whole church is rather than something it sends individuals to do elsewhere, how would it change our life together?
2. Is there a salvageable version of the "key kid" concept?
3. How can we mine treasure from both sides of the evangelical/liberal divide in ways similar to Darrell?

2

Co-Workers in the Gospel

*How Being Apprenticed to Darrell
Guder Transformed My Ministry*

Ross A. Lockhart

NOT LONG AGO I shared lunch with Darrell and Judy Guder at their retirement residence in Seattle, checking in on them both and inquiring about their health, family, and recent activities. I love being in their company, observing how one cares for the other with gentleness and respect. I smiled as they spoke passionately about the most recent book they read or described the latest musical performance they attended. Next, it was a word about the weekly Bible study that Darrell leads for fellow residents, along with an anecdote or two about what the grandchildren were up to. Whenever we are together, I provide Darrell with a fulsome update on the activities of the Centre for Missional Leadership (CML), a ministry of St. Andrew's Hall that is called to discern and equip the future church that God is bringing. Darrell is always keen to hear about the ministry that he helped shape in Vancouver over the last decade, in his role as senior fellow in residence. Like Lesslie Newbigin launching the early missional conversation after returning to the United Kingdom, Darrell's impact on our Presbyterian college and its ministry demonstrates how missiologists can have a profound influence *after* retirement. That day, as we sat in the brightly lit room, and enjoyed a meal surrounded by fellow residents sporting their large name tags, I marveled once again at how this renowned scholar, who I once read and admired from afar in print, had become, over the years, a deeply loved mentor and friend.

Having been apprenticed to Darrell for the last decade, first as the founding director of the Centre for Missional Leadership and then as dean of St. Andrew's Hall, I am grateful for his wisdom and kindness that have shaped my own work and witness in the name of the Lord Jesus. Darrell's influence has stoked my imagination and enlivened my practice of ministry through our ongoing theological discussions, while presenting together at events across Canada and the United States equipping Christian leaders, in various writing projects as well as classroom settings, through entertaining and edifying conversations during long road trips or when breaking bread with others. Darrell's wisdom has been invaluable in navigating the curious mash up of politics in church and academia that we call seminary life, and his encouragement for me to complete a second doctorate (while serving as co-supervisor) in missiology helped transform my ministry as a professor. Darrell's ability to share and show the gospel through his own "worthy walk," reminds me of the apostle Paul's mentorship of folks like Timothy with a commitment to collaborative forms of ministry. In 1 Cor 3:9 Paul writes, "for we are co-workers with others in God's service," and through my apprenticeship to Darrell, I understand more fully now that essential balance of human and divine agency at work in the world highlighted by missional theology. By our baptism into the body of Christ, we joyfully partner with others in a ministry of witness in the world, awaiting the healing of the nations, while participating in the redemptive, revelatory, and revolutionary presence of God: Father, Son, and Holy Spirit.

Missional Church: Where Have You Been All My Ministry?

In my early years of ministry, while still trying to figure out my pastoral identity and developing a meaningful ecclesiology and missiology, I was encouraged by the publication of *Missional Church*. After all, I was ordained into the Mainline Protestant tradition in Canada at a time when one could clearly see the dismantling of a default Christian worldview on the one hand, while still being able to sniff the fumes of Christendom with its accompanying assumptions of privilege, position, and place for the church in Western society on the other. Darrell Guder's work, both as editor of *Missional Church* and his other publications, came at just the right time for my discipleship, when many were unwilling to even engage in conversations about translating the gospel into a post-Christendom West. I recall, for example, asking while at seminary in Toronto where I could take courses on evangelism and mission only to be told in a matter-of-fact way by faculty, "Oh, we don't do that anymore." And yet, as I watched my own Gen X friends walk away from the church while I proceeded toward ordination, I wondered how I might live and lead a Christian life of example in a world where fewer and fewer people seemed interested in the claims of the gospel.

Thank God (literally) that at the same time as I was preparing for leadership in the 1990s for the One, Holy, Catholic and Apostolic church (or reverse those marks if you are an apprentice of Guder) being told that evangelism and mission were no longer relevant, there were scholars like Darrell Guder who were asking the very questions that puzzled me as a young seminarian and pastor. Indeed, the Gospel and Our Culture Network (GOCN) was thoughtfully responding to Lesslie Newbigin's challenge offered in the 1984 Warfield lectures at Princeton Theological Seminary (later published as *Foolishness to the Greeks*) of whether the West could be converted from its growing secularity. Newbigin's central question, which unsettled and inspired the GOCN, could be summarized in this way:

> What would be involved in a genuine missionary encounter between the gospel and the culture which is shared by the peoples of Europe and north America and their colonial and cultural offshoots, the growing company of educated leaders in all the cities of the world, the culture with which those of us who share in it usually describe as modern?[1]

---

1. Newbigin, "Theory of Cross-Cultural Mission." Early North American participants in the GOCN included Darrell Guder, along with colleagues such as George Hunsberger, Wilbert Shenk, Charles West, Craig Van Gelder, Jim Brownson, Alan Roxburgh, and Lois Barrett. Western Theological Seminary, where Hunsberger was on faculty, began to host GOCN activities producing newsletters, contributing to noted journals such as *Missiology*, and interpreting Newbigin's work with the GOCN for the particularities of the North American context with a focus on culture, gospel, and the church. This threefold area of study was further developed in the 1996 edited volume of essays by George Hunsberger and Craig Van Gelder entitled *The Church Between Gospel and Culture*. The favorable response to the ideas raised in the volume set the groundwork with Eerdmans publishing house for future titles in the Gospel and Our Culture Network line, including *Missional Church*.

While Darrell Guder was a respected theologian with distinguished service in church, para-church, and academia in Europe and the United States by the mid-1990s, his name would soon become best known in Christian leadership circles through the publication of *Missional Church* in 1998. By adding the suffix "al" to the world "mission," the authors hoped to foster an understanding of the church as "fundamentally and comprehensively defined by its calling and sending, its purpose to serve God's healing purposes for all the world as God's witnessing people to all the world."[2] Reading *Missional Church* for the first time was a gift and left many of us asking, "Where have you been all of my ministry?" The book articulated what many of us as pastoral leaders were experiencing in the practice of ministry with an urgent need to re-orient Christian communities toward mission in a post-Christendom landscape.

Joining Guder in the Neighborhood

Sixteen years after the publication of *Missional Church*, I moved from congregational ministry to a tenure-track position at St. Andrew's Hall, with a secondment to teach at Vancouver School of Theology. Throughout my pastoral ministry experience in Manitoba, Nova Scotia, Ontario, and British Columbia, I wrestled with what effective Christian witness might look like in an increasingly pluralistic, post-Christendom Canadian cultural context. Fittingly, the board of St. Andrew's Hall discerned that its contribution to the wider theological neighborhood at the University of British Columbia would be a focus on missional theology to bless and equip Christian leaders. I was tasked, in addition to my teaching duties, to establish what became the Centre for Missional Leadership (CML) at our Presbyterian college.

In the early days of the Centre, we met with Darrell Guder, who was approaching retirement at Princeton Theological Seminary, and pitched what I called the "green grass and grandchildren" idea. While Darrell and Judy remained in Princeton, New Jersey, most of the year, we offered to

---

2. Guder, *Called to Witness*, 122. Guder argues that the authors were seeking to explore the implications of Vatican II's ecclesiological and missiological definition in *Lumen Gentium* and *Ad Gentes* that "the church on earth is by its very nature missionary since, according to the plan of the Father, it has its origin in the mission of the Son and of the Holy Spirit." While designed for an academic audience, *Missional Church* received widespread acclaim and attention throughout the various denominations of the Christian church in North America.

fly him out to Vancouver (close to grandchildren in Seattle) in our mild winter months to help build the new CML. To my astonishment, and by the grace of God, Darrell said yes. As a result, in the years that followed Darrell's on the ground presence helped shape and change my pastoral and academic work in profound and lasting ways.

Early on in our work together, Darrell was quick to acknowledge that what the authors of *Missional Church* had meant to convey by their work had actually taken on a life of its own, often with unintended consequences. Today, the language of "missional" has too often become vacuous and compromised by church consultants who repackage "tips and tricks theology" for another how-to manual of "joining God in the neighborhood." However, the core theological claims of missional theology, including the important field of missional hermeneutics, continue to sustain many of us exercising Christian leadership in an increasingly post-Christendom North American landscape.

Over the years, as Darrell and I traveled throughout the Pacific Northwest meeting with pastors, elders, and lay people at CML events, I noted how often Darrell stressed that missional theology is not a fad but rather an important theological argument about the very nature of God's character. We worship and serve a sovereign God who is at work in the world that Christ died to save, enlisting humanity in reconciliation while awaiting the healing of the nations. When teaching, Darrell loves to reference theologian Karl Barth who, in 1932, was already arguing for a greater emphasis upon the missionary vocation of the church and the missionary nature of the triune God that David Bosch later described as changing from a "church centered mission . . . to a mission centered church."[3] Missional theology is far from a recent invention, as Darrell notes that at the Willingen Mission Conference in 1952, the Protestant churches achieved a "strong, global consensus" that the church was missionary by its nature, and that was echoed a decade later by the Roman Catholic Church at Vatican II in the formulation of a missiological ecclesiology.[4] After Willingen, the term *missio Dei* was used more widely to describe the church's

---

3. Guder, "From Mission and Theology to Missional Theology," 43. Guder's own theological convictions were shaped throughout his academic career by the writings of John Mackay, Karl Barth, Lesslie Newbigin, and David Bosch.

4. Guder, "From Mission and Theology to Missional Theology," 43. Guder notes that while Willingen International Missionary Council marked the public event in which *missio Dei* began to form the integrating consensus for mission theology, debate continued for decades later regarding the meaning and impact this understanding had on ecclesiology and missiology.

understanding of the triune God's activity in the world and the church's participation in that mission. This evolution of Christian understanding to both church and mission over several decades shifted the language from "theology and mission" to "theology of mission" to "mission theology" or "missionary theology" as David Bosch described it.[5]

Rather than spending his life in "church consulting," Darrell's contribution to the missional theology conversation has been what I call the "normative/systematic" approach. By this I mean that Darrell's theological thinking, writing, and speaking have helped shaped a new generation of scholarly evangelists, whose words, work, and witness take seriously the *missio Dei*, including the role (and posture) of human agency in the world before an active, sovereign God we know most fully in the redemptive work of Jesus Christ, and the ongoing ministry of the Holy Spirit.

Christendom's Witness Protection Program

Darrell has often reflected with me on his first ministry after returning to the United States from PhD studies and ordination in Germany as theologian-in-residence with the para-church organization Young Life. It was at that time that he wrote *Be My Witnesses* as a way of equipping young Christians to speak and live their faith in a way that demonstrated God's love through the quality of their character. In his early scholarship, Darrell began to name the theological challenges to ecclesiology and evangelism inherited by a modern church steeped in centuries of a Christendom legacy. This includes Darrell's warning of "reductionism" whereby the church trims the gospel to fit the culture, reducing Christian action to little more than a "salvation management system," regulating sin while being consumed with an emphasis on the afterlife. Guder asserts that the purpose of a missional understanding is to "counter the Western reduction of mission, recasting mission as the calling of the church,"[6] while seeking to read Scripture on its own terms for the formation of missionary disciples. In many ways, however, Christendom, with its outsourcing of baptism vows to professional clergy, asked little of members other than to be present (with their presents of an offering) and perhaps to "bring a friend to church," so that the pastor could share the message that would change the person's life. In particular, the Mainline Protestant tradition

---

5. Guder, "From Mission and Theology to Missional Theology," 45.
6. Guder, *Incarnation and the Church's Witness*, xiii.

has often deemphasized the need for Christians to articulate their faith in the wider world, creating something like a Christendom "witness protection program," whereby Christ followers were sheltered from a need to speak to others about core theological convictions. Rather than understanding every baptized believer as a called and sent missionary disciple reflecting Darrell's threefold emphasis on our being (character), doing (action), and saying (words) of witness, the church had too often missed the crucial role of the way in which the Christian community, gathered and scattered, communicates the gospel to a waiting, watching world.[7] Darrell credits Karl Barth's emphasis on witness as significant for his own discipleship, whereby Barth shifted the understanding of a Christian from one who enjoys the benefits of the gospel to one called and equipped for Christian witness."[8]

As the CML gathered pastors, elders, and lay people in retreat and classroom settings, I began to hear again and again some of Darrell's key scriptural touchstones for missional expression. Take Acts 1:8, for example, that helped shape Guder's theological framework for a systematic missional theology: "But you will receive power when the Holy Spirit has come upon you; and you will be my witnesses in Jerusalem, in all Judea and Samaria, and to the ends of the earth." Darrell argues that the early church understood its call to be a witnessing community, with the reconciling gospel of Jesus that was both new and transforming, as well as revolutionary and threatening. That did not change the early church's fundamental sense of their purpose, according to Guder, for Christians were called and empowered to be Jesus' witnesses (Acts 1:8), to "make disciples of all nations" (Matt 28:19).[9] This witness is grounded in the theological understanding of the economic and imminent Trinity's nature, and in his later writings, Guder develops what he calls an approach described as "Trinitarian missiocentricity."[10] By this Darrell means that

---

7. Guder, *Be My Witnesses*, 44. Guder describes Jesus' imperative "to be my witnesses" as a mission statement for the church that is lived out by our being, doing, and saying.

8. Guder, *Continuing Conversion of the Church*, 55. For Barth, Christian witness is in continuity with the Old Testament prophets and the New Testament apostles, who were also biblical witnesses to the word. This redefinition of the Christian life by Barth led Guder to help equip a new generation of leaders in the church to understand that being a witness actually involves the entire Christian life and church, rather than a special skill given to a handful of believers.

9. Guder, *Unlikely Ambassadors*, 5.

10. Darrell likes to say, when using this expression "Trinitarian missiocentricity,"

missional theology grounds local Christian witnessing communities in relational, integrative connectedness to the mission of the triune God and seeks "to integrate theology and practice, out of the conviction that a truly missional church cannot function with a false division between thought and action, being and doing."[11]

The Witness of the Church: Blessed and Sent

As I watched Darrell teach and equip church leaders through the CML, I also noted how David Bosch informed Guder in his normative/systematic approach to missional theology. Bosch taught that mission must be understood as being derived from the very nature of God and placed mission, therefore, deliberately within the doctrine of the Trinity rather than ecclesiology or soteriology for its perceived end goals or outcomes. Bosch wrote, "The classical doctrine on the *missio Dei* as God the Father sending the Son, and God the Father and the Son sending the Spirit was expanding to include yet another 'movement': Father, Son and Holy Spirit sending the church into the world."[12] This sending, in Guder's work, began with the apostles setting up witnessing communities, who, through receiving the Holy Spirit, witnessed to the message among diverse peoples with human beings, through the guidance of the Holy Spirit, incarnating the testimony of the good news themselves, forming and reforming witnessing communities.[13] This missional ecclesiology means that it is God who acts in mission, and the Christian community gathered by this God of action responds by joyfully participating in that same mission.[14] For Guder, "the formation of the community of faith is God's strategy for making the good news known to the world,"[15] and evangelization is, at its core, communication. "It is making the story known. Its intention is not only to tell the good news, but also to invite those who hear to respond and to become part of the witnessing community. Jesus' earthly ministry is the school of evangelization."[16]

---

that missiologists should be allowed to coin at least one phrase, and this is his favorite!

11. Guder, *Called to Witness*, xiv–xv.
12. Bosch, *Transforming Mission*, 399.
13. Guder, *Be My Witnesses*, 113.
14. Flett and Congdon, *Converting Witness*, 5.
15. Guder, *Incarnation and the Church's Witness*, 15.
16. Guder, *Incarnation and the Church's Witness*, 34.

As a co-worker in the gospel, apprenticed to Darrell Guder over these past many years, I have come to understand the catechetical role of witness as a joy-filled practice that helps shape our everyday, ordinary lives as followers of Jesus. God's mission demonstrates a costly love, according to Darrell, where, "God brought about salvation for all creation in the death of Jesus on the cross. That joyful message is now to be made known to all the world."[17] The living out of that conviction, according to Darrell, results in a discipleship that is heavily dependent on divine agency through the Holy Spirit. Guder writes, "Discipleship is not a position, but a call, not an application, but a response, not an end, but an orientation."[18] I am grateful that Darrell has both taught and modeled for me a missional theology that invites Christians into a common calling, responding to God's saving action in Jesus with a grace-filled posture toward the world, offering a hopeful witness to God's weary, waiting, and watching world.

For Reflection

1. Lockhart describes how Darrell Guder's work came at a crucial time in his early ministry, addressing questions about evangelism and mission in a changing cultural landscape. How has your understanding of the church's mission evolved throughout your ministry or Christian life? What challenges or questions do you face in translating the gospel in your current context?

2. Guder warns against "reductionism" in the church, where the gospel is trimmed to fit the culture. Can you identify areas in your own life or in your church where you might be tempted to reduce the gospel message? How can we maintain the fullness of the gospel while still sharing and showing it in today's world that invites others to follow Jesus?

3. This chapter discusses the concept of Christians as "witnesses" based on Acts 1:8. How do you understand your role as a witness in your daily life? In what ways can you embody the threefold emphasis of being (character), doing (action), and saying (words) in your Christian witness?

---

17. Guder, *Continuing Conversion of the Church*, 32.
18. Guder, *Incarnation and the Church's Witness*, 27.

3

Speak Softly and Carry a Pencil

Glimpses of Walking Worthily

Sarah Bixler

Recognizing Missional Distortions

In the spring of 2016, as an incoming PhD student, I was hired to assist in launching a new center at Princeton Theological Seminary (PTS). The Center for Church Planting and Revitalization (CCPR) emerged with a commitment to missional theology as its animating center and the pursuit of ongoing research in church planting and revitalization. Even though it didn't outlive the PTS administrators who approved it, this work sharpened my vocation and clarified my own theology. The primary reason this experience was so profoundly formative for me is because the CCPR director was Darrell Guder, and I had a front-row seat to his theology and how he embodied it in administration.

When I first enrolled at PTS in 2013, I had already heard much about the father of missional theology. Darrell didn't claim that title for himself, but his reputation was well known. I was fortunate to take the last course on missional hermeneutics Darrell taught before his retirement. In that course, I encountered much more than a brilliant theologian. I heard a passionate scholar whose deep love for the church prompted him to communicate with accessible language. I witnessed a well-loved mentor always seeking to carve out space for voices of young and minoritized scholars in the field he developed. I experienced an ecumenical spirit that honored the insights of other traditions, including my Anabaptism. I witnessed a humble follower of Jesus seeking to walk worthily of the calling to which he had been called.

Darrell led the way for the emergence of missional theology as white, Western male scholars recognized a fundamental problem with Christendom's understanding of mission. Christendom had enabled the ushering in of cultural imperialism as missionaries taught the gospel, passing it along in what Darrell recognizes as "the cultural shape of the Western church."[1] In the context of South African apartheid, missiologist David Bosch was similarly noticing how the Western missionary enterprise proceeded from presumed Western cultural superiority and manifest destiny, the theological conviction that Western nations were God's providential bearers of mission to the ends of the earth.[2] My title of this essay is a play on US President Theodore Roosevelt's motto, "Speak softly and carry a big stick." His foreign policy, for which he won the 1906 Nobel Peace Prize, depended on the silent threat of the US military might, a political reflection of the missionary spirit of the Doctrine of Discovery intertwined with Christendom. Over time, Western missionaries may have moved beyond overt physical violence, but their oppressive force of will endured. Bosch locates the origin of the term "mission" in these presuppositions of superiority and control, synonymous with "colonialism" for the last four centuries. In light of this distortion, some scholars have altogether abandoned the study and practice of mission, considering it completely unredeemable.

Yet, Darrell asks the sincere question, was God completely absent and the gospel not encountered during the oppressive centuries of Christendom?[3] Convinced that God's Spirit is not bound by the conditions of human injustice, he seeks to open spaces for truth-telling, repair, and integrity. He embraces the need to confront his tradition's offenses of theology and practice. This necessarily entails a lively discourse about theology and Scripture, in which Darrell engaged throughout his career.

---

1. Guder, *Missional Church*, 4.
2. Bosch, *Transforming Mission*, 305.
3. Lockhart, *Christian Witness in Post-Christian Soil*, 41.

His proposal requires a complete reorientation of many Christian perspectives on ecclesiology and mission: "The church can no longer think of itself as an end in itself but rather as part of God's work of healing and reconciliation of all creation."[4] In light of this ecclesiology, Darrell spoke softly and carried not a big stick, but a humble pencil.

Integration: A Complete Reorientation

Darrell proposed a complete theological reorientation to mission by centering the *missio Dei* at the heart of the church's identity. This is a mission that upholds the dignity of all God's creatures. Darrell's proposals and critiques generated lively scholarly discourse over three decades, which sparked the emergence of the fields of missional theology and missional hermeneutics. Interestingly, the term "missional" caught on far and wide. It is now a lay term—and, as Darrell has lamented, carries meanings far from his original intent. In some contexts, the concept of "missional church" has reverted to the very ecclesiology Darrell critiqued in the first place. The church exists neither for self-perpetuation nor domination, but to participate in God's reconciling mission in the world.

In the fall of his retirement, Darrell gave the 2014 Edwin H. Rian Alumni/ae Lecture at PTS on the annual reunion theme, "Fulfilling the Great Commission." Darrell entitled his lecture "Arguing Christianly: The Practice of Missional Unity in a Divisive Passage."[5] In this lecture, Darrell points out the sad reality that power usually defines unity. Those with social power state the conditions for unity and stand in judgment over those who are forced to comply. This is an act of violence, a terrible form of witness that undermines the gospel of reconciliation, reinscribing oppression in the divisive and domineering conduct of communities that claim Jesus. In our class, Darrell reminded us, "Conduct is the first form of witness. It is not possible for a gospel of healing peace to be proclaimed divisively." Christian proclamation is an incarnational act, and the life of the witness makes the words credible.[6] While arguing Christianly about texts is part of Christian witness, Darrell points out that Jesus only calls his followers to be his witnesses, not judges. Darrell himself exercised

---

4. Guder, "Christians' Callings in the World," 8.
5. Guder, "Arguing Christianly."
6. Guder, *Be My Witnesses*, 27.

this posture of a witness, speaking softly even as he clearly articulated his understanding of the heart of Jesus' gospel.

This illustrates Darrell's early emphasis on the integration of the being, saying, and doing of the gospel. The content of the message and the way it is communicated must be congruent. The life together of the Christian community is the first place of witness and provides the context in which people are formed as witnesses. If the internal life of the community is divisive and riddled with struggles for control, people will be formed as judges or oppressors—the very opposite of the manifestation of the gospel of reconciliation. "If the congregation understands itself a called and sent community," he explains, "then everything it does when gathered relates to how its members function as witnesses when scattered."[7]

These emphases of the connection between the inner life of the community and its outward witness were intuitive for me as an Anabaptist Mennonite. The gift I received from Darrell was understanding why this is imperative theologically and biblically and interrogating the practices of a community that comprise witness. I appreciated learning this kind of critical theological reflection from a Reformed theologian. When I worked with Darrell for the CCPR, he found it humorous to comment in meetings on the providential nature of a Mennonite coming to PTS and assisting with the center. This was a wonderful joke because Darrell knew that I, as an Anabaptist Mennonite, did not subscribe to his Reformed doctrine of providence. Yet the joke generated much more than a good chuckle. It was Darrell's soft-spoken way of inviting a young scholar into theological discourse and affirming my gifts and calling.

Expanding the Basic Hermeneutical Question

It is illustrative that one of Darrell's enduring contributions to the field of missional hermeneutics is not a declarative statement, but a question. Darrell's insight invites further dialogue, offering this question to guide biblical interpretation: "How did this particular text continue the formation of witnessing communities then, and how does it do that today?"[8] In the spirit of refining and extending Darrell's work as he encouraged me and others to do, I propose the penciling in of five additional words,

---

7. Guder, "Christians' Callings in the World," 14.
8. Guder, *Called to Witness*, 92.

reflected in italics: "How did [*the interpretation of*] this particular text continue the formation of witnessing communities then, and how does it do that [*up until*] today?"⁹ Based on the location I inhabit as a female practical theologian informed by feminist and womanist biblical interpretation, I wonder what additional distortions of the gospel become evident when we read texts missionally with added attention to their legacies of interpretation.

Interrogating the legacies of interpretation furthers Darrell's critique of Christendom and adds a new dimension to his hermeneutical approach. The framing of Darrell's basic hermeneutical question may limit interpreters to assuming direct causation and focusing statically on "then" and "today." First, Darrell's question focuses on texts' direct impact on forming communities without a robust accounting for human actors who facilitated people's engagement of these texts. The addition of the dimension of interpretation adds another layer to the historical inquiry and the text's impact on communities today. Additionally, centuries of interpretation lie in between the two points in time of "then" and "today." My added phrases interrogate the legacy of interpretation over time and its formative impact on how Jesus-followers today will answer the basic hermeneutical question.

An Illustration: Interpreting the "Great Commission"

I will offer one illustration of engaging "the interpretation of" addition to Darrell's basic hermeneutical question. The "Great Commission," the theme when Darrell gave the Rian Lecture at PTS, is recognized by both Darrell and Bosch as having a reinvigorated engagement by Western Christendom after 1792.[10] Darrell notes that this text presents a direct challenge to a church that in the age of Christendom ignored it as irrelevant.[11] The text reads as follows (NRSV):

> [18]And Jesus came and said to them, "All authority in heaven and on earth has been given to me. [19]Go therefore and make

9. Bixler, "Great Co-Mission."

10. Ulrich Luz points to a 1792 English Baptist document, "An Enquiry into the Obligations of Christians to Use Means for the Conversion of Heathens," where William Carey points to Matt 28:19a as the central text for missions. Luz, *Matthew*, 626–27.

11. Darrell Guder, "Exploring the Theological 'Why' of Church Planting," in Lockhart, *Christian Witness in Post-Christian Soil*, 41–49.

disciples of all nations, baptizing them in the name of the Father and of the Son and of the Holy Spirit, [20] and teaching them to obey everything that I have commanded you. And remember, I am with you always, to the end of the age."

Bosch goes so far as to call this text "the key to Matthew's understanding of the mission and ministry of Jesus," even while he critiques its irresponsible prooftexting as a mission slogan.[12] Bosch recognizes how this text perpetuated a "subject-object dichotomy" for Western Europeans shaped by manifest destiny who objectified and subjugated persons of other cultures.[13]

Exploring the impact of the interpretation of this text—not just its direct formation of witnessing communities—uncovers layers of oppression in need of reckoning. Womanist theologian Katie Cannon predates the influence of the Great Commission to nearly four centuries earlier than 1792. Cannon describes how the transatlantic slave trade was built on imperialistic interpretations of this passage as a way to hasten *parousia*.[14] As they ravaged the African continent, Western European Christians synchronized enslavement, Christian teaching, and baptism to create a racialized system of human hierarchy where the master's role is to indoctrinate the slave, and any vision for emancipation of the slave is limited to spiritual salvation.[15] The Matthean Great Commission functioned as a hermeneutical key for the logic of European Christian imperialism.

Though the text is literally constructed with disciple-making in the prominent position, its interpretive legacy places emphasis elsewhere.[16] Womanist biblical scholar Mitzi Smith contends that the teaching impulse has overshadowed this pericope's other components, making

---

12. Bosch, *Transforming Mission*, 58, 61.

13. Bosch, *Transforming Mission*, 350.

14. Cannon, "Christian Imperialism and the Transatlantic Slave Trade," 128. Cannon emphasizes Modupe Labode's point that the history of Christianity in Africa should not be confused with the history of Christian missionaries; Christianity existed in North Africa since the time of the early church.

15. "Enslavers tried to indoctrinate Africans to believe that they were duty bound to serve Jesus Christ while they worked for their oppressors" and "help the so-called barbarians grow up in their Eurocentric image, indoctrinating them in their worldview, texts, and languages." Cannon, "Christian Imperialism and the Transatlantic Slave Trade," 131–32.

16. Mitzi J. Smith, "'Knowing More Than Is Good for One': A Womanist Interrogation of the Matthean Great Commission," in Smith and Lalitha, *Teaching All Nations*, 146.

teaching "the primary and essential goal of missions."[17] Botswanan biblical scholar Musa Dube notes the text's absolutist tone, with Jesus holding total authority and commanding his disciples to go to all nations to obey everything he commanded. "Nothing suggests that the disciples of Christ will also need to be discipled by the nations," Dube points out. "Rather, it posits a universally available world, and it advances the right to expand to other foreign nations, to teach them, and to include them without necessarily embracing equality."[18] She argues that this imperialist pedagogical imperative is present not just in the teaching command but is inherent in the broader framework of making disciples.[19]

What Western, English-speaking interpreters envision by the word "teaching" is clouded by centuries of European colonialism in relation to mission contexts where Jesus' gospel message is taught. The problem does not rest with the concept of teaching itself; it lies in its interpretation. Examining the impact of the text's history of interpretation on the formation of witnessing communities, therefore, invites a reckoning with how interpretations of Matt 28:18–20 formed Christendom communities and the impact of that formation today. This recognition opens the consideration of how alternative interpretations might re-form witnessing communities today. This move toward re-formation of witnessing communities will require a reckoning with the past and how it shapes our present. Dube calls "upon both the dominator and the dominated to examine the matrix of past and present imperialism."[20] Dube suggests analyzing the presence of imperialism at all levels by utilizing biblical criticism, sacred stories, oral expressions, and histories from historically subjugated peoples.[21] She also urges scholarly attention beyond a myopic focus on the early church, for instance, to diverse histories and time

---

17. Smith, "'Knowing More Than Is Good for One,'" in Smith and Lalitha, *Teaching All Nations*, 127.

18. Dube, *Postcolonial Feminist Interpretation of the Bible*, 137.

19. This imperative transgresses national borders in order for someone with superior knowledge to inform and "lift up" those in an infantile position. Musa W. Dube, "'Go Therefore and Make Disciples of All Nations' (Matt 28:19A): A Postcolonial Perspective on Biblical Criticism and Pedagogy," in Segovia and Tolbert, *Teaching the Bible*, 224–25.

20. Dube, "'Go Therefore and Make Disciples,'" in Segovia and Tolbert, *Teaching the Bible*, 234.

21. Dube, "'Go Therefore and Make Disciples,'" in Segovia and Tolbert, *Teaching the Bible*, 236.

periods.[22] These interpretive strategies suggest how an examination of the interpretation of this text could form witnessing communities today for greater faithfulness in the being, doing, and saying of the gospel.[23]

Carrying a Pencil

When I assisted Darrell in the administration of the CCPR, I spent many hours alongside him in networking meetings. It was a fascinating opportunity to learn and observe, and he made a point to invite me as an equal voice into conversations with church leaders, entrepreneurs, and theologians. During these meetings, he would often set a follow-up appointment. He would open his paper calendar and pull out a pencil, but occasionally, he forgot to bring one. The first few times this happened, I offered him the only writing utensil I carried—a pen. "Thank you, but I only write appointments in pencil," he would say. "That way I can change them as needed." As I watched him fill up his weeks and months with penciled-in appointments, I came to recognize that this was not just an approach to calendar keeping. Darrell ordered his life, work, teaching, scholarship, and theology around the assumption that they were all open to change. The pencil became a metaphor for the way I understand Darrell's posture in the world. So, I started carrying a sharpened no. 2 pencil with an eraser in my own bag, for the pleasure of sharing it with Darrell when he needed one.

In addition to carrying a pencil, Darrell speaks softly, both in literal and figurative terms. He offers his insights with clarity and humility. I will never forget my experience of being present for Darrell's last day of teaching at PTS. Much to Darrell's surprise (which is another testament to his humility), administrators and faculty joined our missional hermeneutics class to mark the end of Darrell's long legacy of teaching. It was a celebration and a mourning all at once. Many sincere words of appreciation were offered, and then Darrell was invited to respond. He was overcome with emotion. The only utterance he managed was this soft-spoken acknowledgment: "I am a teacher because of my students." In honor of Darrell and all he taught me, to this day I still carry a pencil in my bag. Every time I see it, I am inspired to walk more worthily of the calling to which I am called.

22. Dube, *Teaching the Bible*, 243.
23. Guder, *Be My Witnesses*, 133.

For Reflection

1. Darrell Guder emphasizes a reorientation of the church's mission to focus on the *missio Dei*. How does this shift in perspective change the role and identity of the church in the world?

2. Reflect on the importance of congruence between the message of the gospel and the way it is communicated, as emphasized by Darrell Guder and experienced by Sarah Bixler. How can this principle be applied in contemporary Christian communities?

3. Bixler notes how Guder's teaching highlighted the relationship between power and unity within the church. How does the misuse of power undermine the gospel of reconciliation, and what steps can be taken to foster genuine unity in Christian communities?

4

Creational Theology Is Missional Theology

JONATHAN R. WILSON

Both God's act of creation and God's determination to heal his rebellious creation are the compelling reason for the salvation history which unfolds from Abraham onward.[1]

What makes the gospel truly good news is the fact that the Jesus events are the outcome of God's loving decision to heal the broken creation. We have described this as God's mission. To demonstrate divine love, God brought about salvation for all creation in the death of Jesus on the cross. That joyful message is now to be made known to all the world. That is how God's mission now continues.[2]

---

1. Guder, *Continuing Conversion of the Church*, 32. Guder is aware of the criticisms of the term "salvation history" and notes that he is following the missional use of the term by Johannes Blauw (*Continuing Conversion of the Church*, 29n3). My exposition intends to show that the "missional salvation history" centered in the particular story of Israel and Israel's Messiah is the "salvation history" of all creation.

2. Guder, *Continuing Conversion of the Church*, 49.

If the (missional) church that Darrell Guder has so passionately and faithfully advocated is going to bear faithful apostolic witness to the gospel in the coming years and decades, we must recover the biblical *narrative* of God as Creator and a *narrative* account of creation.[3] Amid all the questions that are being asked today about the environment, sexuality, economics, and competing ideologies, the Spirit is guiding us into a rediscovery of the story of creation from Gen 1–2 to Rev 21–22. We have often had these two "bookends" to the gospel, but the story that we have told has often passed quickly over Gen 1–2 and begun the story with Gen 3, setting aside the original goodness of this world. This is a devastating mistake that strips the good news of its fullness and distorts the church's mission.

In this essay I will begin with a reading of Gen 1–2, especially 1:26–31, as missional theology. In other words, I will argue that my reading of Gen 1–2 identifies the original and continuing missional mandate of God's people. This may seem to challenge dominant readings of Genesis 1–2 as a creation or cultural mandate, with a "missional mandate" arriving later. But as I unfold my reading of Genesis, I will show that my reading embraces the whole biblical narrative and finds its fulfillment in Jesus's co-missioning his disciples in such passages as Matt 28:18–20.

My reading of the story of Scripture begins with Gen 1–2, but I will continue from there to show that "creational theology" is *the* story. It is not one act in a three-, five-, or seven-act drama. In those readings, "creation" is often simply the beginning of the drama or the setting of the stage for the drama: "creation" simply announces the birth of the cosmos, like a biography may begin by announcing the date and place of the subject's birth and his or her ancestry. There is some insight to be gained from this analogy, but I will propose a reading of Scripture that teaches us to use "creation" to refer to more than the beginning of the cosmos. I will show that Christians should use "creation" to refer to the web of life at the center of which is Jesus Christ, "through whom and for whom all things were created" (Col 1:16). Creational theology as missional theology is

---

3. When Darrell and I shared an office at St. Andrew's Hall, UBC, we had several conversations about Karl Barth's theology and some mistranslations in *Church Dogmatics*. We recognized that like Karl Barth (and Lesslie Newbigin), we share a passionate commitment to being faithful to the gospel *and* being wise in discerning the times and the particular demands of witness in our times. In this essay, I bring those two commitments together for today and for decades to come.

thoroughly and persistently a *Christocentric* narrative of creation. At the same time, because it is Christocentric it is also Trinitarian.

Re-Reading Genesis 1:26–31

If we read the narrative of this passage within the context of Gen 1–2, we can identify five relationships that constitute the life of creation. These five relationships then become constitutive of the entire narrative of Scripture: the story of creation, a story with several chapters in which each chapter continues and unfolds the story to its end. Genesis 1–2 is the beginning of the story, the weaving together of five relationships that constitute life.[4] And God said, "Let us . . ." This passage reveals four of the five relationships at the heart of creation.[5] The fifth will come into view as we continue the story into Gen 3. The first relationship is the proleptic pointer—"Let us"—to the Trinitarian God who is self-sufficient as one God in relationship as Father, Son, and Spirit.[6] The second relationship is between God and human creatures. We are made by God.

We are spoken to by God. When God speaks, God *blesses* and *commissions*. We may even say, "Creator blesses *by* commissioning." The third relationship is among human creatures. How else can we be fruitful and multiply? But as we anticipate the continuing story, this does not mean that every human relationship must be procreative. What it *does* mean

---

4. F. Leroy Forlines, professor of theology and Bible at Free Will Baptist Bible College, first introduced me to "four relationships" in a course on biblical ethics. My development of them is very different from his. My addition of a fifth relationship, now my "first" relationship, distinguishes my account of the "web of life" from "Gaia's web" (Bakker, *Gaia's Web*). The life of Creator is not circumscribed by the web of creation. By identifying this "first" relationship in the narrative, it is clear that God *is*, prior to creation and mysteriously more than creation.

5. My account bears some affinity with "relational" accounts of the *imago Dei*. But it differs in two ways. First, it broadens the relational account to include the "web of life." Secondly, it depends not on some putative meaning of the Hebrew words translated "image" and "likeness," but on the *narrative*. Most accounts of the *imago Dei* overload the simple phrase with a burden it cannot bear. Moreover, we *must not* universalize any one account of the *imago Dei* such that *we* are empowered to determine who is made in the image and who is not. Such a semantic overload and universalizing may easily lead to euthanasia and genocide.

6. I acknowledge that the scribes who preserved and taught this text understood it as a "royal we" or as God speaking in the heavenly council. But the fuller sense of Scripture teaches us to read it today as Spirit-infused anticipation of our coming to know God as triune.

is that in our relationships with other human creatures, we are commissioned to nurture life and the community of human creatures. The fourth relationship is between human creatures and the larger creation. We are to fill the earth and "master" it.[7]

We must be careful here to read this commission as part of the narrative of Gen 1–2. In Gen 1, Creator fills the earth. The human mission to "fill" the earth must be understood in light of this prior filling. Linked to the command to multiply, "fill the earth" certainly means that we should populate the earth. But read together with "master it," fill the earth is also a call to oversee the fulfillment of the earth according to Creator's purpose. Thus, "master it" does not mean "impose your will upon it." Master farmers do not impose their will on the land. They do not insist on planting rice in soil and a climate that won't sustain a crop. Master farmers *cultivate* the land and adjust to the conditions of soil and climate so that life—the life of their part of creation—may flourish.[8] This account of the relationship between human creatures and the larger creation is confirmed in Gen 2, where the earth creature is to work the garden and guard it.

There are two more important aspects to the story at this point. First, human creatures are assigned to care for and even "master" the earth, *but* their own lives depend upon the earth providing the food that they need to live. Humans do not live "above" the earth; they come from and depend upon earth. In God's economy, the earth itself is life giving. Here is reciprocity though not symmetry. Secondly, these relationships are genuinely a web in which all members of the web connect with all the others.[9] We cannot separate the relationships from one another. God is related to the human community, the larger creation, and broken selves. The human community is related to God, the larger creation, and broken selves. The same web of relationality is true of the larger creation and broken selves.

In Gen 1–2, the first "people of God" are co-missioned to live in, care for, depend upon, and extend the relationships that are the web of life.

---

7. Here I am following the translation of the JPS Tanakh.

8. As I write this during the summer of 2024, "stone fruit" growers in British Columbia are quickly pivoting away from stone fruit because of changes in the interior climate of the province.

9. I have been working with this image of "web of life" for several years now. I only recently discovered that Terrence Fretheim uses the same image. See Chan and Strawn, *What Kind of God?*, 187–205.

This creational mandate is *the* missional mandate. In fact, my proposal is that when we read Gen 1–2 rightly, there is no distinction between a missional mandate and a creational mandate.

Re-Reading Genesis 3–11

In Gen 3, the web of life—the harmonious, life-giving relationships among Creator, earthlings, and earth (the larger creation)—is torn apart. The humans hide from Creator; the man blames the woman (and implicitly God); they will increase and multiply in greater pain; and they will now wrest their life from the earth instead of receiving it as a gift.

It is here that a fifth relationship comes into view: a relationship of the earthling with his or her self. In Gen 2, the first humans are naked and unashamed. In Gen 3, they become "self-aware" and they seek to cover their nakedness. They are ashamed of themselves; they are broken selves.

The following chapters, Gen 3–11, trace the effects of this tearing of the web of life in every relationship. These chapters proleptically and summarily tell the story that has been lived throughout history and is still being lived today. It seems that there is nothing new under the sun.

Re-Reading the Story of Israel

But there *is* something new. In Gen 12, Creator begins the work of re-weaving the web of life by calling one man. The promise to Abram echoes the beginning of creation in the web of life. The "mission mandate" given to the first humans in Gen 1–2, is now given to a new people of God, Abraham and his descendants. Abram is promised a covenant relationship with God, a people (be fruitful and multiply), a land (master the earth and fulfill its purpose), and blessing. This is not the beginning of a new mandate or a story discontinuous with Gen 1–2. It is the continuation of the original mission of the first people of God under different conditions (a chaotic and violent world) and requiring new resources (Torah and its formative practices).

We can see this mission throughout the OT. Recall, for example, how the "Ten Words" describe the reweaving of relationships among God, humans, the larger creation, and the self. The case law that follows on these Words shows concretely and strikingly the integral nature of the life and mission of the people of God. Recall also how this web of life is *integral* to the Psalms and the message of the prophets. Broken selves turn away from God and, in their covetousness, oppress other humans as a consequence of which the land languishes and does not provide what is needed for life.

At the same time, however, the psalmists and the prophets assure the people that God is faithful to the covenant and will continue to reweave the web of life if they will turn back to God. The mission of Israel as God's people is to fulfill the mandate given in Gen 1–2. The web of life is not whole but broken, and Israel must be transformed and taught how to participate in the web of life that Creator is reweaving. Yet the mission is the same: live in harmonious, life-giving relationships among Creator, earthlings, the larger creation, and self. This is the missional mandate of the people of God.

But the OT people of God fail in their mission. When they fail to participate in the reweaving of the web of life, the prophetic voice rings out against their attempts to please God with fragments of faith and mutilated practices. Their worship of idols, their immorality and injustice toward others, the infertility of the land, and the fearful, proud, broken selves are the consequence and evidence of the broken web of life.

In the OT, the people of God undergo a long and painful tutorial in the consequences of their failure to participate in the reweaving of the web of life. But that same tutorial also prepares the way for the One who reweaves the web of life: Jesus the Messiah, the Master Weaver, the one "through whom and for whom all things have been created" (Col 1:15–20).

In brief form, consider the following:

1. Jesus lives in unbroken relationship with the Father and the Spirit. This unbroken relationship is summed up in "I and the Father are One" and "The Spirit of the Lord is upon me."[10] These statements and others only have meaning and reference within the story of Jesus. In Christ, our relationship with Creator is rewoven.

2. Jesus reweaves human relationships. The healing of people's bodies reweaves their relationship to the larger creation *and also* reweaves them into the social fabric of human relationships. These "miracles" are not primarily proof of Jesus's divinity but signs that the web of

---

10. To these representative statements we may add such statements as "I do only what I see my Father doing" and "The Spirit drove him into the desert" and "If you have seen me you have seen the Father." These few statements should remind us of many more and, more importantly, as noted in the text, of the narrative of the NT.

life is being rewoven. New creation! And it is here that we are co-participants in the work that is often identified as "justice." But this justice, as our participation in the reweaving of the web of life, is God's justice accomplished in Jesus Christ and continuing in his name today.

3. Jesus reweaves our relationship to the larger creation. Above we noted the effective reweaving of our relationship to the larger creation in Jesus's acts of healing. He also reclaims the rightful human mastery of creation in his calming of the storm. In his feeding of the four thousand and five thousand, he reverses the curse on the land and exposes the false fear of scarcity that breaks our relationship with the land through exploitation and abuse. In the Master Weaver's feeding of the thousands, as in Gen 2, the earth yields life to humans as a gift, not as an agonistic extraction. And in his embrace of children might we see a deep reclaiming of the original blessing: "be fruitful and multiply"?

4. Jesus reweaves our relationship to self by always being nothing less and nothing more than who he is. The first place we see this is in his resistance to the Tempter in the wilderness. Among many dimensions to the temptations, one is to betray who he is—to adopt an identity other than the one he has in relationship to the Father and the Spirit. We may also observe his undivided self in his responses to the many challenges to his identity and authority. (I won't multiply references here; rather, I will trust readers to recall these passages or to search them out.) When we come to be "in Christ," we are already made whole, restored to the telos of a healed, undivided self—a "new creation" that is more than a reinstatement of the original creation. There is "something more" in the Word becoming human and reweaving us into the web of life. In Christ, we are healed and whole—that's the story of the redemption of creation in the human. But there is also the continuing story of the broken web, and in this story, which ends only in our death or the return of Christ, we are in the process of being healed and made whole.

This full reweaving of relationships is "finished" when the Incarnate Word is crucified and raised from the dead. This "event" of Jesus the Messiah is an unfolding of and witness to the meaning and significance of Jesus Christ for all creation, which Paul declares in Col 1. This reweaving also calls into being the NT people of God: those who are being rewoven into the web of life and whose mission is to bear witness in word and deed to the good news that all creation has been woven back together in and through Jesus Christ.

The People of God

In the same way that God called Abraham and made him a nation to learn the reweaving of the web of life, the reweaving of the web of life creates and co-missions a people to prolong the incarnation, that is, "prolong" Jesus's reweaving of the web in the world today.[11] Given the story of creation as the weaving, tearing, and reweaving of the web of life, the mission of God's people is clear. Our mission is holistic—integral—embracing all of the web of life. Our witness to this good news in word and deed is fragmented and distorted when we "specialize" in one or another of these relationships. Or even two of them. Or three. Creational theology as missional theology requires us to prolong the Incarnation through witness in word and deed to the reweaving of the whole web of life.[12]

How this integral mission is carried out is different in Thessalonica, Ephesus, Rome, Vancouver, Kumasi, Bruges, Tianjin, Beirut, Cochabamba, Adelaide. Here the Trinitarian grammar of mission is our guide.[13] The Father sends the Son to reweave the web of life—this is the mission. The Son fulfills that mission. The Spirit creates a people who continue that mission. And the Spirit is the "missionary" who leads the people of God in their work of prolonging the incarnation. In the particular "contexts" where the people of God find themselves—however large or small that context—those contexts, *in their very particularity*, are redeemed by the larger, cosmic reality of the reweaving of the web of life.

---

11. I have adopted the language of "prolonging the incarnation" from Ewell's *Faith Seeking Conviviality*, 67–68, 81, 91, 189, 219, 227, 260–63. "Prolonging the incarnation" is different from "incarnational mission." The former phrase maintains the unique, once-for-all act of the incarnation of the word as Jesus Christ. The latter threatens to obliterate that uniqueness by calling on us to somehow imitate the incarnation, which is theological nonsense.

12. Darrell has pioneered the identification and correction of the "reduction of salvation and mission" in Western Christianity. I intend for my narrative account of creational theology as missional theology to assist in correcting our vision of the gospel.

13. For the practice of "Trinitarian grammar," see Wilson, *God's Good World*, ch. 5.

Creation Care

To bring this to a concrete point of co-missioning, I will focus on "creation care," or how we are to be the people of God amid multiple environmental crises. There are three primary responses to these crises: despair or apathy; denial; technological hubris. Creational theology as missional theology shows us another way. The reweaving of the web of life shapes our mission and witness in at least three ways.

First, we know that the future of creation is God's new creation—a making new of all things that God has made through God's work, not ours. So we do not despair of our weakness and poverty; rather by caring for creation we bear witness to this sure hope in all things re-newed.

Secondly, the reweaving of the web of life shows us that the brokenness of the web of life affects all relationships. We should listen and learn from climate scientists, but God's people should not need them to tell us that the larger creation is torn away from the relationships that give it life. To deny the crises in creation that we humans have wreaked is to deny the biblical story, not climate science.

Third, we can bear faithful witness only as we do the difficult work of understanding how our broken relationships infect any attempt to "solve" the environmental crises through human skill and ingenuity alone.[14] Nor can we regard "creation care" as a concern for our relationship simply with flora, fauna, soil, water, and air. We must pursue creation care within the web of life. We must act now but we must act with humility in faithfulness to the One "through whom and for whom all things have been made."

Creational theology as missional theology shows us that the third way is faithful, forceful action that begins with the healing of our relationship with the Creator. Only the Creator can re-new this creation. Creational theology also shows us the way to repentance—from all the ways that the broken web is embedded in our desires, our actions, our thoughts. Creational theology calls us to a relationship with the larger

---

14. I am thinking here, for example, of Bill Gates, *How to Avoid a Climate Disaster: The Solutions We Have and the Breakthroughs We Need*. The same reliance on human control is conveyed by the title of Katherine Hayhoe's *Saving Us: A Climate Scientist's Case for Hope and Healing in a Divided World*. Hayhoe is a top climate scientist and evangelical Christian whose voice needs to be heard inside and outside the Christian community, which makes the implication of the title doubly wrong. But I also think that my work may be a complement to Hayhoe that offers more theological depth and a clearer warning that in our action, we must act with humility and wisdom rooted in the fear of the Lord.

creation rooted in the humility of wisdom that itself is rooted in the fear of YHWH. Such wisdom does not seek to control but to understand, cultivate, and protect.

Creational Theology Is Missional Theology

If we are to be faithful to Scripture and understand our mission as the people of God today, we must recover the full biblical narrative of creation from origin to fulfillment. *In the beginning*, God's first people are given their mission. *In Israel*, God forms a new people to learn and participate in that mission under new conditions and with new resources. *In Jesus*, the mission becomes Christologically focused and given to God's people, who by the presence and power of the Holy Spirit participate in and bear witness to the reweaving of the web of life. The hope and joy and peace of *all* creation is the life and witness of the missional people of God.

For Reflection

1. The author argues that our proclamation of the good news and our understanding of the mission of the church should be shaped primarily by Gen 1–2 rather than Gen 3. What practical difference would that make in your own life and thought and in the mission of the church and its proclamation of the good news?

2. Imagine that you are talking to a family member, friend, or neighbor who is very open to Christianity. How would you present Jesus as the "Master Weaver" in your own words in a way that they might understand?

3. What concrete difference might the argument of this chapter make in your life and the mission of the church or Christian organization that you are most familiar with?

5

A Unique Partnership
Young Life and the Lutheran Church of Württemberg

CHRISTOPH SCHNEIDER

DARRELL GUDER IS BEST known for his impact on the missional church conversation in North America; however, Darrell's ordained ministry and early formation were lived out in Germany in the early Cold War years. Darrell's ecumenical approach to ministry bore fruit even before he returned to North America. Indeed, an example of this was the partnership between Young Life International and the Lutheran church of Württemberg, in the southwest of Germany, officially started in November 1975.[1] Darrell Guder had been teaching at college in Ludwigsburg, Germany, for several years when he became the catalyst

---

1. While Darrell is primarily known for his contributions as a missiologist, he has been committed to the support of youth evangelism organizations, the so-called parachurch. Prior to his decade-long tenure with Young Life International in Colorado, Darrell had been teaching at a seminary in Germany in the early 1970s. During this time Darrell helped orchestrate the launch of a Young Life chapter in southwestern Germany, one which will be celebrating its fiftieth anniversary in 2025. This essay seeks to reflect on how Darrell helped shape this organization, particularly through equipping its leaders for incarnational witness. There are countless people and organizations who have been impacted by Darrell, in North America and beyond. What follows captures how some of the ripples of Darrell's life and witness continue to impact people today, and into the future.

to the formation of what is now known as the Young Life Partnership. Bringing together two unlikely groups, past president of Young Life Bob Mitchell once commented, "This was unheard of, that a youth organization in the United States would have a real live dynamic partnership with a European church body, like the Lutheran church. It's an unbelievable marriage!"[2]

During the early 1970s both Darrell and the church of Württemberg were concerned about connecting with the youth and young adults who were no longer involved with Christian groups. While many children were raised in the church, and went through confirmation, by the age of fourteen or fifteen, the vast majority of youth were no longer attending church. Darrell has reflected on this situation, noting, "At the time—I was there until 1975—I would say 25% of the youth population was involved in a Christian youth program—either Protestant or Catholic."[3] Not content to only focus on the 25 percent of youth who were still involved with the church, Darrell began to ask: *What about the 75 percent who were not? How do we reach our own young people evangelistically?*

Darrell identified that the key challenge to connecting with the youth outside of the church was about evangelism. Drawn to the church of Württemberg, with its very strong evangelical tradition and profound concern about the challenge of its own younger generation, Darrell began to wonder about a partnership with Young Life. With Young Life's focus on going outside the traditional forms of the church, the structure of the parish, this partnership had potential.

Although an unlikely partnership, Bob Mitchell noted, "I'll bet there isn't anything in Christian history that compares to it—a crazy, wild, laid-back organization like Young Life, in partnership with a staid, traditional, government-sponsored, liturgical church. It has to be in the providence and good humor of God, that it ever came about."[4]

The Development of the Young Life Partnership

To reach the young people in southwestern Germany, Darrell's incarnational theology and witness were a strong inspiration for the partnership. However, not one to provide an answer and prescribe a plan, Darrell

---

2. Char, *German American Partnership*, 4.
3. Char, *German American Partnership*, 16.
4. Char, *German American Partnership*, 2.

initiated discussion between the two groups to help answer the question of how to reach young people evangelistically. Therefore, at the very beginning of the partnership a theological consultation of people of the Lutheran church of Württemberg and Young Life staff, including Darrell, took place. The main question was, "What does all this talk about incarnational witness, incarnational ministry, incarnational evangelism mean?"

Three themes stood out as important from these discussions. First, with respect to incarnational witness, personal encounters were important, especially answering the question, "What is my very personal history as a disciple of Jesus Christ?" Second, the organizations needed to account for the different understandings of ministry identity for those involved with youth ministry versus the institutional church. Third was the need for an exchange in methods and methodical experiences, particularly, when answering the following questions: "How can the church's witness take place in a secularized world? How can the church best reach the unreached? How can the witness of Christ be passed on in many forms which correspond to the many different groupings we encounter?"

From this consultation it was identified that the most important method of Young Life is the life and the attitude of the leader. Darrell reflected on this, saying, "So we began to talk about a theological understanding of evangelism which is rooted in—not only the message, but the life of Christ, as a way of doing evangelism. Lifestyle as evangelism."[5]

To elevate the strategy of the life and attitude of the leader, Darrell introduced the concept of incarnational theology to the partners. New to them, at the time, incarnational theology meant the incarnation of God in Jesus, the inspiration of Scripture, and the identification of the Lord with his disciples today.

This understanding of incarnational theology then led to four questions which were theologically relevant regarding the church's witness: First, what is the understanding of interpersonal relationship which is derived from the gospel? Second, what is the effect of this understanding on the person of the disciple and on his attitude toward other people? Third, what concrete ways of behavior result from this understanding and this attitude? And fourth, how can it happen that these behavioral patterns develop a dynamic through which other people are led to faith in Christ?

5. Char, *German American Partnership*, 14.

The Impact of Incarnational Witness

Darrell's contribution with the idea of "incarnational witness" went far beyond this small partnership in Germany. Reflecting on the development of the partnership in Germany and his own theological contributions, Guder wrote:

> The theological contribution is very real. In fact, out of the German dialog came ultimately the design for our course in "Theology of the Incarnational Witness" in the Young Life Institute, because we didn't have a theological language in Young Life that we could use. I'd have to say that my own book, *Be My Witnesses*, (1985) on incarnational witness has come out that exchange.[6]

At that time Young Life was observing that a lot of staff were apologetic of our style when they went to churches and Bill Starr (president, Young Life 1964–78) didn't want them to feel apologetic. He remembered: "Someone told me about Darrell Guder, and I sensed Young Life needed someone who was more theologically oriented. He talked about the diaconic orders in the church of Württemberg and invited me to 'come and see.'"[7]

Later Bill Starr brought Darrell back to the United States to be part of the training department of Young Life. The partnership, and Darrell's personal influence, impacted Starr's life significantly: "One of the things that came out of the Partnership for me was the desire I had when I moved to Minneapolis from Colorado. I really wanted to demonstrate what I thought could be done for Young Life and the Church." Therefore, Bill initiated pastors' fellowship groups and first pastors' conferences at Trail West Young Life Camp.

Darrell Invited and Connected People with "Come and See"

The impact of Darrell's theology and invitation to "come and see" can be felt in this organization even today. "Come and see" was also my own personal invitation into the partnership with Young Life and the Lutheran church in 2009. I was hired by the youth organization of the church of Württemberg to develop a "partnership-youth-ministry-project" with

---

6. Char, *German American Partnership*, 42.
7. Char, *German American Partnership*, 5.

the intention of moving from institutional church youth ministry to missional church youth ministry. At that time, I had just followed the invitation of "come and see."

I would say the frame of "come and see" is the invitation to show incarnational witness.

Already during my first days of being in the partnership I was introduced to the talk about incarnational witness, incarnational ministry, incarnational evangelism, and what all that means today. I'm still fascinated that there is a God, who became flesh in Jesus and lives among us.

During my research on Darrell's experiences in the beginning of the partnership I found a lot of similarities to the challenges we face today. Secularization continues and youth are still leaving the church around the age of fourteen or fifteen. A local pastor told me that only four young people signed up for confirmation class in his parish, out of the thirty-two who were invited, and these were young people whose parents were members of the church.

Obviously, the question Darrell asked at the beginning of the partnership is still relevant for my work today: *how do we reach our own young people evangelistically?*[8] This led me to start a "Young Life Training Academy" for full time youth workers in the church to be inspired by the idea of being a witness and living incarnationally. The Academy is all about being a disciple, based on Mark 3:13–15: "Jesus went up on the mountain and called to him those whom he desired, and they came to him. And he appointed twelve (whom he also named apostles) so that they might be with him, and he might send them out to preach and have authority to cast out demons." Being with Jesus and being sent out to bring good news to the world—that is the calling.

First, the Academy is all about the *personal encounters*. The questions to be answered are the same as in the beginning of the partnership: What is my very personal history as a disciple of Jesus Christ? How can I be near Jesus in my daily life? Or how can Jesus be near to me? We encourage people to find their personal spiritual forms and times of being with Jesus.

Secondly, we look at what it means to be the *sent ones*. This reflects the encounter between those with different understandings of the identity of those in youth ministry. What does it mean that the church is primarily the assembly of real persons in a real place in the name of Jesus

---

8. Char, *German American Partnership*, 15–16.

Christ? What does it mean for staff people to carry out discipleship and servant leadership? We encourage staff and volunteers to be a witness and live a lifestyle of being sent to others in order to invite them personally rather than to just offer groups to join.

Finally, we ask, how can we do and live this on a daily basis? This reflects the exchange of methods and methodical experiences. How can the church's witness take place in a secularized world? How can the church best reach the unreached? How can the witness of Christ be passed on in many forms which correspond to the many different groupings we encounter? We encourage people to live an authentic Christian lifestyle, which means not every method is authentic with every person. That leads us to use a variety of methods, with a unity in mind and heart of being a witness of Jesus Christ.

Darrell's Inspiration Is Still Alive in Our Context Today

The movement is still going on in Württemberg, and the most current mission statement of the Young Life Partnership is inspired by the understanding of Darrell's incarnational theology and desire to follow the *missio Dei*. Our vision is that every young person would have the opportunity to be transformed through an encounter with God. Christ and relationships are our two values which support this vision, by employing four processes: contact, community, connection, and commission. Our desire is that these four processes will be represented in our diverse programs, events, offerings, and expressions, such as youth groups, camps, clubs, leadership teams, sports teams, and confirmation groups. We are excited about all those who join us on this journey, as we seek to reach every kid.

Even today, Darrell's teaching and life have had an impact on the people of all generations within this partnership. Darrell laid the foundation stone for this partnership which is still alive. Even more important is that Darrell introduced us to and inspired us by the idea of *lifestyle as evangelism* and living as *incarnational witness*, both of which we are still using to convey and communicate at our camps and our daily youth work.

In fact, while I was writing this essay, my eight-year-old son Tomek came home from school and showed me the gift he got at the church service for the end of this school year. It was a bracelet that says "Dich schickt der Himmel" (You are sent by heaven). Isn't it that, what Darrell means by this Jesus-lifestyle we are still "walking worthily"? Let us live our lives as a gift from heaven, like Jesus, as we are reminded in Phil 2:5–11. In closing, I am humbled by the thousands of people that have been impacted and influenced by Darrell through the Young Life Partnership, either directly or indirectly. As Darrell brought an attitude and awareness of being a witness of our Lord Jesus Christ, I offer this blessing with gratitude for his life and witness:

> Der HERR segne dich und behüte dich;
> der HERR lasse sein Angesicht leuchten über dir und sei dir gnädig;
> der HERR hebe sein Angesicht über dich und gebe dir Frieden.
> Amen.

For Reflection

1. What were the main challenges that Darrell Guder and the church of Württemberg faced in connecting with youth and young adults during the early 1970s? How did these challenges shape the formation of the Young Life Partnership?

2. How did the concept of "incarnational witness" influence the partnership between Young Life and the Lutheran church of Württemberg? What are the key elements of this concept as discussed in the chapter?

3. How did Darrell Guder's theology and the idea of "come and see" continue to impact the partnership and the broader mission of Young Life? What lessons can be drawn from this approach for contemporary youth ministry?

6

Para-Church Ministries

Parasites or Partners?

David J. Montgomery

The extensive missiological and ecclesiological output of Darrell Guder has been an undoubted gift to the world church. As a Presbyterian minister and a para-church leader, I can identify with many aspects of his own journey and have found his thinking and writing both accessible and enriching. His burden for "the church to be the church" and his vision for post-Christendom congregations are profound in their implications and catholic in their application.

An Inevitable Tension?

Guder speaks from the inside, *as* a church person *to* the church. He also speaks as one with inside experience of the para-church having served as Young Life's theologian-in-residence. Certainly, in his critique of the contemporary Christian landscape, the para-church ministries do not appear unscathed. Guder interprets the proliferation of various para-church agencies (along with the fragmentation of mission into separate ministries within many churches) as owing more to corporate business philosophies and methodologies than to a biblical ecclesial vision and is concerned that evangelism-oriented agencies, in particular, too easily become reductionistic in their ecclesiology and even their soteriology. Furthermore, he writes: "The problem is often compounded when such evangelistic organizations ultimately start 'local churches' for their converts, in competition with Christian communities already in place, thus dividing the church and its witness even more."[1]

To those of us who are committed church people and have spent a large proportion of our lives also serving in para-church ministries, we may struggle to relate to this tension. To us it may be self-evident that the para-church serves the church, and the church is enriched by the para-church. We may be clear in our minds that our para-church ministry is not a church, and should never claim to be, and that starting a new para-church ministry cannot be perceived as "church planting." We may insist that those we work with should be plugged into a local church, and that the local church should likewise support the complementary work of the para-church.

However, not all see it this way. For the purposes of this chapter, my paradigm for the para-church will be that with which I am most intimately familiar: national and local student groups operating on campus under the banner of IFES.[2]

I am aware that both students and church leaders have, at times, seen the ministries of church and para-church as at best independent and at worst competitive. On the one hand, for students who have discovered in the para-church a vibrant fellowship and effective mission which is providing a discipleship and a depth of spiritual life they have not found in their local church fellowship, it is easy to denigrate the church and to believe that the student group *is* their *de facto* church.

On the other hand, church leaders, regardless of their ecclesiology, can easily point out the shortcomings of this argument. If they have a high ecclesiology, they will highlight the fact that mono-generational campus groups do not have any form of regular governance, cannot exercise discipline, and cannot (or should not) practice the sacraments.

---

1. Guder, *Continuing Conversion of the Church*, 136.

2. The International Fellowship of Evangelical Students is a global fellowship of autonomous national student movements in over 160 countries. See https://ifesworld.org/en/. It was formed in 1947 through the amalgamation of existing movements in ten countries, some of which had already been in existence for some decades. Each national movement has its own name and structure. The North American affiliate movements are InterVarsity (USA), InterVarsity (Canada), and Groupes Bibliques Universitaires et Collégiaux du Canada.

Others of a lower ecclesiology will concede that in many ways the campus group is a group of believers gathering round God's word as a witnessing community and is therefore effectively a church. But, they argue, it is church done poorly without mature leadership, and it would be better if they put all their well-meaning efforts into the mission of a local church under the authority and oversight of that church's leadership.

When I was a student in the United Kingdom[3] a few decades ago, this tension was largely invisible. I participated in and led my campus group during the week, and on Sunday I and my fellow students were regular attendees at a local church. There I joined in fellowship, worship, outreach and even cut my teeth preaching. That local church was an active supporter of the campus ministry, praying for us, encouraging us, and most importantly feeding us after the service! In addition, the pastoral staff provided much needed counsel for me whenever my own stumbling efforts at leadership were landing me on rocky ground.

It may have been that at that time there were fewer churches, certainly outside the major cities, who shared the missional vision of the para-church. While many pastors may have had such a vision, it was often aspirational, and they struggled to bring their congregation with them. In contrast, they saw the enthusiasm and evangelistic zeal of the students as an example of what they were trying to engender within their own congregation and therefore were happy to support it.

However, in the intervening years, and not least through the work of writers and practitioners such as Guder, increasing numbers of churches have re-caught the vision and are functioning as vibrant missional communities in university towns and cities. Therefore, the question has arisen: has the para-church outlived its purpose? This of course is not just a question for university ministry, but for any mission agency. Are local, national, or global para-church evangelistic agencies necessary when so many churches are now grasping an incarnational understanding of church life and witness which is expressing itself through their own structures, in the form of local and international programs? Are social justice organizations required when so many churches, large and small, are setting up their own food banks, drop-in centers, debt counseling services, along with pregnancy, postnatal, and bereavement counseling?

---

3. Having lived and studied in both North America and Europe, I am aware that Guder's critique is largely directed at the North American context and is prompted by the sheer proliferation and duplication of para-church ministries evident there. His general theological concerns, however, are more universally applicable.

Few would deny the need for specialized organizations to undertake the work that churches cannot do themselves (e.g., Bible translation, research, and publishing,) or provide an outlet for gifted Christians across the traditions to collaborate (e.g., theatre and the arts). The question is who should initiate this and what relationship should they have to church structures?

While some of the tensions mentioned earlier could be put down to pettiness or territorialism, a much more robust critique of the para-church has been offered by Guder. Based on his understanding of the church's holistic mission being indivisible from the church as an incarnational community, he fears that the gospel proclaimed by para-church or specialist ministries will inevitably be reductionistic.

> Further evidence of the reductionism of the church and its mission that must issue from a reductionist gospel is the emergence of organizations often called para-churches. This nomenclature originally meant that they were Christian ministry organizations "next to" the established and traditional forms of the church. Although that definition is still valid, there is a prophetically accurate reduction in the prefix, since it implies that the evangelistic mission of the church can be separated out from the rest of the institutional church and function as its own distinctive ministry.[4]
>
> The gospel proclaimed by such movements must necessarily be reductionistic, because it is separated from the incarnational witness of the mission community. . . . When evangelization is divided from the incarnational witness of God's people in community, the danger is very great that the gospel will be reduced to the minimum of personal salvation and private faith.[5]

Guder's critique is welcome, if a little too generalized. It is a timely reminder that the *raison d'être* of any mission agency cannot be separated from, or exist in isolation from, the work and mission of the church. It is not difficult to find examples where this is the case, but does it have to be so and, as Guder claims, does the gospel proclaimed in these contexts *necessarily* have to be reductionistic?

---

4. Guder, *Continuing Conversion of the Church*, 136.
5. Guder, *Continuing Conversion of the Church*, 191.

The Problem of Definition

As Guder indicates, a foundational issue is the problem of definition. The term *para-church* is problematic because it easily separates the specialist ministry from the church: too much "para" and not enough "church." "Para/alongside" infers that the two entities (the agency and the church) run on parallel tracks. Para-church advocates would argue that they are not parallel to the universal church, but *part* of the universal church and their members are a part of local churches.

To call such ministries *inter-church* can also be misleading, as it implies a formal ecumenical body under the authority of existing cross-denominational leaders. Some have suggested *intra-church*[6] (i.e., arising out of the church and ministering back into the church). This is more accurate but is not an easily understood term.

Writing in the context of student ministry, Mike Reeves, in an on-line article,[7] proposes a more helpful vocabulary. He gives a summary of the biblical and historical evidence for specialist ministries outside the strict parameters of a local congregation and, following Ralph Winter,[8] he suggests reintroducing the term "sodality" (from the Latin for "fellowship"). While this also is a lesser-known and not easily understood term, Reeves shows how it has a rich history, and once understood, it can be helpfully applied to a ministry such as IFES. He writes:

> It was the traditional term used in the early post-apostolic church to refer to all the non-congregational fellowships of believers (such as the monastic communities). The sodality was a voluntary fellowship which would be formed within the larger community for a more precise, focused and limited task than the whole community could attempt. Instead of distinguishing between the church and the "para-church," with the theological confusion that can all too easily follow . . . [we should refer to] the local church and the sodality.

---

6. This term was suggested in an unpublished paper by Rory Press, general secretary of SCO, the South African affiliate movement of IFES.

7. All Reeves quotes are from this unpaginated article: Reeves, "CU and the Church." Reeves is the former head of theology at UCCF, the British affiliate movement of IFES.

8. Winter, "New Missions and the Mission of the Church," 89–100. If "modality" is the traditional, all-encompassing community of the church, then sodalities are the specialist intentional ministries. Guder acknowledges this differentiation (*Continuing Conversion of the Church*, 182–83).

He illustrates how in certain contexts (e.g., university campuses) sodalities are better placed and equipped to minister than local churches. He also points out the role of sodalities in the ongoing renewing of the church and how, as sodalities became more effective, they drew criticism from the church hierarchy who wanted to control them. When this happened, it almost always led to the theological dilution of the mission and a spiritual decline. Therefore, where there has been a tension in the relationship, it has not always been initiated by the sodality. In my context it is true that, at times, the relationship between church and IFES has been viewed as either independent or parasitic.

Independence is often the comfortable choice of some students, possibly even endorsed by some para-church staff or executives. They think the church is too dead, or too small, or too big, or not missional enough, or not Spirit-filled enough, and the para-church groups or cohorts therefore don't need the church; they can survive well enough independently. It is clearly not a biblical view of the church, and any healthy para-church ministry should eschew this, encouraging its members and insisting that its leaders attend and serve in a local church.

Parasitic is the accusation mentioned earlier, often leveled at para-church ministries by church leaders. Just as a parasite feeds off the larger organism, so student groups can suck the life out of a local church through its members being so active on campus that they have no time for church, yet they expect the church to support them and therefore the church is deprived of their energy and enthusiasm and they end up being a "net drain" on the church's resources: putting nothing in, but taking lots out. If the para-church student ministry was not there, the argument goes, the church would be stronger. Of course, the para-church will say that they are working and witnessing where the church cannot go (in this case, on to campus or into a faculty building) and that praying for and supporting such ministry should renew and rejuvenate the church's own missional vision.

And so, while recognizing that these criticisms leveled at both the church and the para-church may not be without substance, I propose that, building on the idea of the sodality, there is a healthier way to envisage the relationship:

Symbiotic is a term which Tim Keller helpfully uses to describe the relationship between evangelism and social concern in his book

Ministries of Mercy,[9] and it is applicable here. It refers to how two organisms grow and renew themselves through being interdependent. The local student fellowship is the missionary arm of the church on campuses. The local church will benefit from the witness of the student fellowship and could even see it as part of its own mission to support practically those members who are working with the fellowship. The church, in turn, can provide a stable, worshiping, intergenerational, discipling fellowship for the students.

What If?

Of significance to this discussion, however, is Guder's concern that para-church organizations, particularly those whose focus is exclusively evangelistic, are likely to have a reductionistic gospel. While this is not unknown, it is important to take into account, not just the breadth of the gospel, but also the breadth and diversity of the para-church sodalities.

So, what if a sodality's work is focused on something a local or even national church does not have the resources to do? What if it has an ecumenical vision beyond one denomination or expression of church, allowing believers of multiple traditions to work together toward a common goal? What if an essential dimension of the sodality's evangelism and discipleship is full integration of the new believer into a local community of faith and they work hand in hand with multiple churches to ensure this happens smoothly?[10] What if the gospel being proclaimed in the context of the sodality is not limited to personal salvation, but incorporates whole-life witness and the application of gospel truths to all of society?[11]

---

9. Keller, *Ministries of Mercy*.

10. NKSS, the Norwegian IFES group, have a regular pre-term event where they invite pastors and leaders of a broad range of churches to attend. This enables students to find an appropriate local church into which they can be integrated while they are at university and makes a statement from the beginning that NKSS and the local pastors are in partnership.

11. For example, IFES's vision is "to see students thriving together as communities of disciples, transformed by the gospel and impacting the university, the church and society for the glory of Christ" (IFES, "Our Global Vision"). IFES global ministries include Engaging the University, https://ifesworld.org/en/university/ (see also Good News for the University, a European initiative, https://www.goodnewsfortheuniversity.org/); also Graduate Impact, https://www.graduateimpact.org, which, among other things, initiates "city groups" across the globe, bringing together Christian graduates

Posing these questions, I believe, will keep the sodality alert to the danger of reductionism, but will also help the church to have a more accurate understanding of how the work done in theologically strong and spiritually rich sodalities can enliven the local communities from which their members come and to which they return.

One further question, I believe, needs to be added to the discussion. Namely, what is it that only the church can do? Guder is correct in his critique regarding the proliferation and duplication of para-church agencies and the divisive force that that can be, often over-stretching the resources of local and national churches. I attend many gatherings of para-church staff and am often struck at how the work of many of those agencies could easily be incorporated into the ministry of a local church; equally I have attended church gatherings, be they open days, local councils of churches, even general assemblies or synods, and asked, "How much of the work done by these ministries, sub-groups, or committees, could be done (usually better) by non-church agencies, and would our members not be better being salt and light co-operating with local community efforts rather than seeking to replicate them within a church context?"

If it can be the case that para-church sometimes usurps the work of the church, is it also not the case that sometimes the church can be found replicating the work of civic society? This is not a call to reinstate some sacred/secular divide: on the contrary. If it is the role of the church *in diaspora* to live the gospel wherever they are planted, let them contribute meaningfully to local business and politics. Meanwhile let it be the work of the church *in ecclesia* (in both its modalities and sodalities) to be an incarnational worshiping community.[12]

---

in law, economics, politics, arts, history, etc. These groups allow Christians from different traditions to tease out the vocational implications of the gospel together, complementing the work of their respective local churches.

12. The concept of church *in diaspora* and *in ecclesia* is outlined in Paul Stevens, *Liberating the Laity: Equipping All the Saints for Ministry*. While this in itself runs the danger of artificially separating the witness of the church, the distinction is helpful, particularly when it comes to understanding the respective roles of the church as a body, organization, or institution, and church members in their daily context or "frontline." For the concept of "frontline ministry" see Hudson, *Imagine Church*.

Toward True Partnership

I have been privileged to work in churches that have acknowledged the blessing of sodalities, not just in terms of student ministry, but also in terms of theological training, crosscultural mission, political advocacy, to name just a few. I have also been privileged to work for a sodality that takes seriously its indebtedness to and contribution toward the health of the church. While sodalities may be administratively independent, they can never be spiritually independent.

Specifically, there are a number of ways in which a para-church group and the church can serve each other, and thus grow stronger. Using student ministry as our example, while the task of pastoring and discipling young believers rests primarily with the local church, this may also be undertaken synergistically by church-supported organizations who can train a generation of students, especially those whose churches are not willing or equipped to engage in such ministry, thereby serving the church by preparing students for future congregational involvement and leadership.

There are many ways in which local churches and the para-church can and do work together. For example, when I was in parish ministry, I experienced firsthand how the local church benefited from vibrant campus groups in the neighborhood. Students were involved as local church members; they were nurtured in the early stages of their faith in an interdenominational and international context, expanding their horizons beyond the confines of a particular local or denominational fellowship; they received "on-the-job" training in biblical interpretation, spiritual leadership, proclamation, apologetics and dialogue, and conference-planning, and a few were also given organizational experience by serving on a national board or chairing a national student council. Unsurprisingly, a very high number went on relatively quickly to serve in church leadership. They were encouraged and equipped to be bold in communicating the gospel in the hostile environment of the secular university and offered advice in how to respond to opposition and exclusion graciously, preparing them for potentially similar challenges in the workplace and society; in some cases they were mentored in how to navigate politically complex situations, both internally or externally: a skill that is often undervalued or naively dismissed in congregational life.[13]

---

13. For more on how important, yet neglected, the issue of political intelligence is in church life, see Burns et al., *Politics of Ministry*.

Yes, in some quarters, there will be students who don't think they need the church, and churches who don't think they need a student ministry group active in the local university, or possibly who feel threatened by it. The former need to be discipled, but perhaps some local church leaders who have an enthusiastic student ministry on their doorstep could be encouraged to see the benefits of partnership and their responsibility as local Christian leaders to nurture and not to discourage such zeal to reach the campus with the gospel.

Meanwhile, those of us ministering within the campus sodality need to continue to be committed to reaching skeptical students with the transforming news of Christ, training them in all the implications of the gospel and ensuring that they are integrated from the beginning into an incarnational, intergenerational church community.

For Reflection

1. What are the main tensions identified in this chapter between para-church ministries and traditional church structures, and where have you seen those tensions in your own experience?

2. In what ways can para-church ministries and local churches collaborate more effectively to avoid competition and fragmentation?

3. What role do you believe para-church ministries should play in the broader mission of the church?

Missional Theology Shaping Specific Communities

7

Living the Missional Call

Thomas Daniel

It is impossible to measure the impact of Darrell Guder on the church in North America. His writings and teachings have shaped a generation of pastors, para-church leaders, ministers, and theologians. However, I want to reflect on the alignment between what he teaches and how he lives. It is said that true leadership is not telling others what to do, but it is doing something yourself and inviting others to join you. He has been that kind of leader to so many and I am grateful to be one whose life has been forever shaped by Darrell Guder.

To show the magnitude of Darrell's presence in my life and ministry, I need to share a little about my background. I grew up in a very affluent family in Atlanta, Georgia. Like most respectable families at the time, we were regular attendees at church. My parents had decided to leave the Southern Baptist denomination during the civil rights movement and migrated to the more progressive Presbyterian church. We were very involved there when I was a child. My parents both served on Session and taught Sunday School, and my mother even chaired a capital campaign for a building renovation.

There was, however, nothing about faith in any of these religious activities. We never prayed as a family or talked about God. I don't remember ever seeing a Bible in our house. Church was simply an activity that was expected of respectable people, and we met that expectation without fail. However, when I became a teenager, I had no interest in waking up on Sunday morning and my parents decided that I could stop attending. So, starting around age fifteen, I began staying home most Sunday mornings rather than accompanying the family to church.

This pattern lasted until I was eighteen years old and about to begin my freshman year at Davidson College. Throughout my senior year of high school, my father had been a member of an Associate Pastor Nominating Committee for our congregation. One June evening, my parents were in the middle of an intense argument when my father announced to my mother, my two younger brothers, and me that he had been involved in a romantic relationship with a woman serving on the Nominating Committee and that he was moving out of the house that night and would begin the process of divorcing my mother. Outside of the devastation to my family, this had the effect of cementing any sense that I had about the validity and importance of "church." It was a useless and hypocritical organization which would have no place in my life.

And that is where it remained throughout my tumultuous college years. Upon graduation from Davidson, I was accepted into a teaching program in Japan called the JET Program that is run by the Japanese government. Every high school and junior high school in the country has a native English speaker on staff to teach conversational English to both students and faculty. I was assigned to the prefecture of Fukui, which is the most rural area on the main island of Japan. It turned out I was the only Westerner in my village, called Mikata, and this meant that the regional network of English teachers in Fukui became a lifeline of relationships for me. Local teachers would gather on weekends to spend time together in what was a wonderful, but often lonely, time of teaching in the rural towns and villages throughout the region. One day a fellow teacher on the JET Program from Ireland, Donna McDowell, announced that she had been attending a local charismatic church and was getting baptized. She invited many of her fellow teachers to attend, I was one of them, and experiencing Donna's baptism changed my life forever. There was something spiritually alive about the tiny congregation, called the Bunkyo Gospel Center, and I was drawn to the vibrancy that was evident when you walked in the doors. That is where I eventually became a

Christian and God completely reoriented my life and worldview. In the end, I lived in Japan for two years, met my wife, Beth, a fellow teacher on the JET Program, who is Welsh, and became a follower of Jesus. It took me leaving the Bible Belt and going to an Irish woman's baptism in a charismatic Japanese congregation to encounter the person of Jesus.

After two years in Japan, Beth and I decided to move to America as I wanted to study more about this new (to me) Christian faith, and growing up in Atlanta, I knew of a school where this could happen—Columbia Theological Seminary. Beth and I moved on to campus in August of 1998. What followed was the most disorienting period of my life. My assumption had been that all of the students and faculty would have similar experiences and outlooks to mine about Jesus, the Holy Spirit, and the power of conversion. It turned out, however, most of the students and faculty had grown up in the Presbyterian church, had never left, and could not relate to my conversion. I remember one person telling me they were "suspicious" when they heard my story about coming to faith in a charismatic house church in Japan. Within a matter of days, I felt completely lost and Beth and I decided that we had made a mistake in showing up at this mainline institution. I was looking at dropping out and trying to discern what our next step would be when I heard a lecture from a man I did not know, Darrell Guder, and it spoke to my mind and my heart as nothing else had.

I do not remember everything Darrell taught that day, but I do specifically recall how he explored the conversion of Saul on the way to Damascus in Acts 9 and how this moment was the beginning of his calling to be sent to the gentiles. Right from the start, Darrell affirmed the power of God to invade a life in the most powerful of ways, for a person to be totally reoriented, and that conversion was the beginning a life spent in witness to others. He emphasized that conversion was seen by many people of faith as the "finish line," but biblically it was the "starting line." At the end of his lecture, he took questions from both students and faculty, who pushed back on some of his interpretations, and he answered them with intelligence and humility. I left that class with a purpose—to get to know Darrell Guder.

That very afternoon I stopped by Darrell's office without an appointment. He was sitting at his desk. I remember how nervous I was when I knocked on the door. It was clear from the lecture that Darrell was a person of extraordinary intelligence and wisdom. I quickly came to realize that his intellect is partnered with a disarming kindness. He introduced himself, invited me to sit down, and wanted to learn more about my journey to seminary. For about forty-five minutes he gave me his full and undivided attention and I spoke without pausing for breath. I told him about my family of origin, my disappearance from the church in America, my coming to faith in Japan, my sense of the Holy Spirit, and my complete confusion about my experience in seminary. I told him I was looking at leaving at the end of the semester. Darrell patiently listened and then asked if I was free for breakfast the next morning so that we could talk more. He invited me to his home, a block from campus. The next day, I rose early, walked to Darrell's house, and enjoyed a breakfast of toast, jam, and tea. We spent ninety minutes visiting in more detail. What I vividly recall was the way Darrell affirmed my story, validated the unique ways that God was at work in my life, and talked to me about how my experience of God and the church would be a part of my missional calling for years to come.

That breakfast was a turning point for me. Suddenly I had a person who did not make me feel as though I had to apologize for my journey. We began having a standing weekly breakfast together for almost three years, until Darrell left for Princeton Theological Seminary. Our weekly conversations and friendship were of utmost importance in my life and development as a follower of Jesus. Darrell was the first person who ever prayed with me, challenged me about how to grow as a leader, and was vulnerable in allowing me to know how I could pray for him. He got to know my wife and invited Beth and myself to spend time with him and Judy. I was first "discipled" by Darrell Guder and whenever I read his books, or hear him lecture, I see the same man who met with me in his home week after week. Missional theology is not Darrell's area of expertise so much as it is an expression of how he lives his life. I hope to emulate Darrell's example daily.

In my current context of Austin, Texas, twenty-five years after first meeting Darrell, I continue to lean on all that he has taught me. It has been an incredible gift to our congregation to have him visit on multiple occasions to preach, teach, and interact with our leadership. On one visit, Darrell invited us to think about ways to measure "success" as a missional church rather than an attractional church. He used a phrase in this lecture: "Covenant Presbyterian Church is called to be a love letter from God to the city of Austin." This phrase captured the imagination of Covenant and we have spent years discussing what it means to be a love letter from God. This image has given rise to several initiatives: providing medical debt forgiveness, hosting forums with elected officials, asking how we can mobilize our congregation to partner with local government. The idea of being a "love letter" has become a commonly used phrase at Covenant through the years.

However, Darrell also challenged us that being a love letter requires more than just increased programming. It requires us asking about the goals of our overall formation process as a congregation. We therefore had a group think about what it meant to encourage our people to consider being a love letter on a daily basis wherever we live, work, and play. This led to the creation of the "Love Letter Fund" in which people can apply for funding to experiment with missional initiatives. The only people who can apply are our members and they can pitch ideas about how they want to live as witnesses to their faith. Recipients have included a small group of accountants who used the funds to start a microloan initiative with Afghan refugees in Austin. Another enabled a restaurant owner to employ refugees from Africa who require extra assistance with learning English and opening bank accounts than the workers that would have been hired had the funds not been available. In these instances, the members of Covenant did not need to do this work, but the fund allowed them to experiment with how to think a little more about ways their vocations could be used to live out a missional calling from God. And these initiatives have caught the attention of the local press, and therefore, many of our neighbors who are not Christian. We have been able to conduct open dialogues about the unique joy that comes from knowing and following Jesus. And the results have been stunning. The vast majority of our growth in recent years has been among women and men who were not part of a church before coming to Covenant.

The refugees impacted by the Love Letter Fund will likely never know the name Darrell Guder. Neither will the thousands whose medical debt was forgiven, nor the folks who have been baptized as new Christians. But make no mistake: he has been an important part of each of their lives. They have all been blessed by the life, faith, and work of Darrell—included in the living legacy of this wonderful man. And so have I. Darrell was a love letter from God to me when I was lost and directionless. What he gave me was not contained in his job description as a seminary professor. It would not be rewarded in any annual evaluation. And what he offered was so important—not a book or podcast to consider, but the gift of himself. It has changed me forever.

For Reflection

1. Thomas distinguishes strongly between being a member of a church and being discipled by another Christian. The former can inoculate against following Jesus; the latter was essential to the author coming to faith. Who has discipled you the way Darrell discipled Thomas? Whom have you discipled?

2. In mainline churches we do not often narrate our coming to faith (arguably in evangelical churches such narrations happen all too often). Should we do so more often? If so, how?

3. What would it mean to think of your church as a "love letter" to your city? How would that change how your church makes its life together?

8

For the Beauty of Chestermere
Darrell Guder and the Proximal Imagination

PRESTON POUTEAUX

FOR OVER A DECADE I've served as a pastor in one of Alberta's most fascinating and headline-making communities: Chestermere. While our community certainly made the news for hosting the World's Longest Hockey game to raise hundreds of thousands for charity, or for becoming Western Canada's first Bee City, one Google search will reveal sorrow, struggle, and disorder in our beautiful lakeside community.

We made national news recently when the provincial government of Alberta took the unprecedented step of removing our city's mayor, three councillors, and three city executives. Our city had been governed in "irregular, improper and improvident manner" and the tone of political discourse collapsed to such an extent that it required a team from our province to step in. The minister of municipal affairs said, "the people of Chestermere deserve better."[1]

Our city now wrestles with rapid growth and a significant vacuum of social infrastructure. Chestermere has over thirty thousand people, but we do not have a hospital or high school in our city limits, no long-term care home for seniors, homeless shelter, funeral services, or even a

---

1. Ellis, "4 Chestermere City Councillors."

hardware store and swimming pool. Our community, for its size, also has the fewest places of worship or Christian organizations of any city in Alberta, according to the Cardus Institute's Halo Project.[2] As a pastor in our community, I lean in and wonder: what is the "better" our community needs in this season? What vision or imagination of hopeful neighborhoods, good governance, healthy Christian community, and thoughtful civic discourse can grow in this place?

How do we respond to the anxieties that take root around us? I continue to observe that burdens of responsibility are often pushed off to another level of government or agency. We have found ways to blame distant forces and systems, seeing much of our shared challenges as beyond our control. We see these conditions emerge among us, so we push back from each other. With every angry hot take or protest we become removed, above and away from others. We shake our heads from a safe distance and tweet our frustrations out into the world. While the comments sections rage on and fractures deepen, trust erodes and soon we wonder why a widening void has taken the place of our once shared hope.

Darrell Guder, and the missional conversations he curated and wrote about, came to me at a time several years ago when I began serving the least churched city in Alberta. I had big questions about how we could work for the good of this place. How could we be a church that is a sign, servant, and foretaste of the kingdom of God? I could see Darrell Guder pointing in a direction, but it wasn't until I began to live this missional posture, drawing near to others, that I started to understand that he was pointing to the beautiful presence of Jesus in my midst.

It was in this place of wondering that I also stumbled into the garden. My wife and I were turning a barren suburban patch of land into something that actually grew, and we came alive with our hands in the soil. While she was sketching out designs for a new edible garden to be planted just above our rockery, I was getting into beekeeping. It was a calm and elderly neighbor that took me into his apiary for the first time. I offered to help him with his bees, but it was his gentleness that taught me a valuable missional lesson. As we donned our protective beekeeping equipment, he opened the hive to me. There, before me, were thousands of honeybees. It took my breath away. Would they sting? Was I safe? How could I possibly manage? Then, with the kind wisdom of a seasoned teacher, my mentor began to explain that beekeeping is a posture. Gentle

---

2. Halo Project, "Halo Effect."

proximity to the bees is what makes a beekeeper. You must draw near, and the bees will teach you and reshape your imagination. They will give you signs of health and sickness, and in time you will know how to care for them, but you have to lean in. Listen. Touch. Wait. Act. Maybe even love them.

The first season of beekeeping seemed utter chaos to me. Sweating in my bee suit I was hot and found myself frustrated, I'd get stung, my hands were sticky, and I couldn't see through the veil. Bee boxes were heavy and a frame full of honeycomb would break in my untrained hands. I certainly had many moments where the romantic notions of beekeeping and creating beautiful thriving gardens felt far off in the disorder of my own learning. But my mentor knew that through the chaos and complexity, I would learn to love the bees and tend to the bees—all by being close to the bees.

Darrell Guder offers a proximal imagination for the church today. His body of work is a cogent invitation toward a consistent leaning in, and drawing near, to the tender work of the Spirit in the church and world. Like a seasoned mentor, he invited me out and down from my safe vantage point to see the way that the church engages in the mission of God. My discovery: leading the church in times of chaos requires that we get far closer in order to love far more deeply.

Guder's work was, for me, a twofold invitation. First, he offered an invitation toward Jesus. Our formation begins by being close to Christ, becoming like Jesus, and doing what Jesus invites us to do. Guder writes, "Here is a definition of discipling that . . . invites the Christian community into a relationship of intense personal formation, a process of discipleship paralleling the three years of schooling of those first followers of the Rabbi Jesus. The outcome in every instance is to be a repetition of Jesus' ministry with these disciples."[3] A proximal imagination for our formation looks like the stories we see in the Gospels; we are formed as we gather around tables to allow the words and kingdom actions of Jesus to become ours, and to live in response to the death and resurrection life of Christ.

The second invitation was toward my neighbors. This is, for Guder, a way that we indeed "walk worthy" of our calling. How we live in proximity to our neighbors, whoever they may be, reflects how we live out a biblical and missional vocation. This proximal imagination makes little

---

3. Guder, *Called to Witness*, 128.

sense if it remains a mere idea; it sprouts to life as we draw near to others. He writes, "The command to love will cease being an abstraction or a sentimentality as the community learns the concrete actions that express God's love for us. God's love toward us is translated immediately into the practice of love that followers of Jesus are enabled to have for each other."[4] Guder locates disciples in proximity to Jesus, as those watching and imitating him. This posture then translates into a movement toward real, actual neighbors. It is here that he says that "we are taught by him, through the word, that our neighbors are the people we cannot avoid, the people we have to deal with, the unsightly and unseemly who are stretched across our path and whom we have to go to great lengths to walk around. We learn that we are sent to our neighbors, that our mission field begins with those next to us."[5]

The missional imagination that Darrell Guder offers only seems to make sense when we move in close proximity to the life of Jesus, and to the life of our neighbors. Even the structures of our churches "will always emerge out of the interaction of the gospel with the cultural context."[6] Our vocational calling makes sense only insofar as we are able to be very close to what it is we are called to love. We can hardly call a bee enthusiast a beekeeper until they have experienced the chaos and frustrations of tending to real, actual bees. We can hardly call ourselves the church if we have not walked with Jesus into the hard and complex neighborhoods we are called to love.

The beautiful presence and work of the Holy Spirit will be evident in our cities when we draw near to "the unsightly and unseemly" people who are before us. This language, although sharp, certainly captures the hesitation we feel when we think about our own cities and the broken and fractured pieces we find around us. If we consider the failures of our municipalities, neighborhoods, churches, or communities with a Jesus-formed proximal imagination, we find ourselves standing on holy ground. We begin to see, and bear witness to, the deep and transforming work and presence of the Holy Spirit in our midst. The work of God, though cosmic in scope, becomes human in scale. The mission of Jesus becomes haptic. We realize that we can reach out to touch, knowing the redemptive living and loving presence of God is the key that turns over

---

4. Guder, *Called to Witness*, 153.
5. Guder, *Called to Witness*, 153.
6. Guder, *Missional Church*, 227.

the shame and fear barring our communities. In the hands of God, borne in God's people, present and near to the world God loves, we can begin to see even our neighbors as central to God's story.

Two years ago, I was invited to become the Royal Canadian Mounted Police (RCMP) chaplain for our city. This role welcomed me to draw close to the complex and hurting stories of crime and sorrow in our community. Early on as I was being oriented to the local detachment, the sergeant who invited me to take on this role pulled me aside and said, "Preston, I don't think you should do this." Surprised, I asked why. He said, "You love this community a lot, I'm afraid if you see the dark underbelly, you'll lose some of that love." I thanked him for his care and simply said that I think you love something even more when you see it at its worst. Never have I felt closer to my city than when I drive around in the middle of the night with our RCMP members stepping in and out of the hardest moments we share as a community. It is in proximity that we see the sorrow, and it is in proximity that we imagine how to love.

The mission of God may be even more intimate, still. Darrell Guder invites us to engage with the early Christians to see the tenderness of their mission. He writes that the congruence of their faith "took the shape of a gentle, nourishing, caring self-giving in relationships illustrated by the image of a mother nursing her child."[7] This kind of intimacy was not a new strategic master plan; it was a posture of maternal love. He goes on to say that the "love that Christian community members practice toward one another enable[s] the demonstration and explication of that love as good news to their neighbors, those next to them, and those to whom they are sent." It is here in this intimate nearness that, like a mother and child, we can begin to imagine the shape of our own cities and neighborhoods again. No longer as places of separation and isolation, but the beginning of self-giving care and gentleness.

In gentle wisdom Darrell Guder welcomed me to look again at the sorrow, chaos, and challenge of my own place in order to draw closer with a new imagination for the mission of God, the good news of Jesus, and the divine reality of the gospel. The kingdom of God "is coming and is now very near,"[8] he would say. May we live anew into this proximal imagination, guided by the Holy Spirit, to see and touch our neighborhoods

---

7. Guder, "Walking Worthily," 266.
8. Guder, "Walking Worthily," 269.

with the love and tenderness of Christ. Thank you, Darrell Guder, for showing the way, and inviting us to sit a little closer.

For Reflection

1. In this chapter Preston writes about the divisions that grow in our communities, "With every angry hot take or protest we become removed, above and away from others." How do you see separation as a sign of deepening ill-health in your community? What forms does it take?

2. Preston frequently compares his work as a pastor and community caregiver to beekeeping. He calls his early experiences of beekeeping "chaos" that made him frustrated. How have your efforts to tend to your place, even close up, created frustration for you? Why?

3. Preston quotes Darrell Guder, saying, "The command to love will cease being an abstraction or a sentimentality as the community learns the concrete actions that express God's love for us." What freedom could be found for you beyond the abstractions and sentimentalities we experience at a distance? What challenges in your community could very well be met by moving into closer proximity? At what scale does Jesus work in these challenges?

9

Tents and Tabernacles

Albert Y. S. Chu

Back in 2004, I moved to Richmond, British Columbia, with the prospect and hope of planting a church. At that time, church planting was still caught up in the throes of Christendom. Enamored by the success of megachurches such as Willow Creek and Saddleback, church plants relied on people still seeing the church as a desirable place to come and find God. The overarching strategy was to get people to come to a church worship gathering of some sort whereby they would be engaged in a culturally relevant fashion.

I remember going to a weeklong church planter training workshop in Orlando, Florida. For some reason, they called it a Church Planter's Boot Camp, which naturally raised the question of "who exactly are we fighting?" The Boot-Camp manual and curriculum encouraged us to have good signage, use mailouts, play contemporary music, offer bagels for breakfast, and whatever you do, do not use fancy theological words in the sermon! I remember one site pastor of a large megachurch; when asked where he found inspiration and creativity, his response was . . . wait for it . . . Disneyland. It took me a minute to realize that he was NOT joking.

Disneyland? Is this what I signed up for?

My hope was to plant a church, not a worship service with smoke machines and fancy lights. Nor to plant a safe haven for Christians looking for a new holy huddle. I wanted to plant a church that would be a place of welcome and hospitality for those in my neighborhood, and to weave diverse people into the fabric of a loving community (hence why we named the church plant the Tapestry). I wanted to find fellow sojourners to pray with, share meals with, do life with, and to be sent together into God's harvest field. Isn't that why we plant churches?

Enter Darrell. As I continued to struggle against this attractional model of church planting, I began to hear people use the term "missional" for the first time. The ideas that Darrell and others developed through *Missional Church* were a breath of fresh air. It was encouragement that I desperately needed to hear. I came to discover that to be missional was a paradigm shift of how I understood the very nature and character of God. God is a missionary God. God the Father sends God the Son and God the Spirit to redeem and reconcile all things. Among the many things I came to realize was that to be missional was to move beyond a narrow definition of mission. Much too often, we have relegated mission to be one among the many different programs of the church. And not even the most important, with worship often understood as being the primary function of the church. As Darrell writes:

> It has taken us decades to realize that mission is not just a program of the church. It defines the church as God's sent people. Either we are defined by mission, or we reduce the scope of the gospel and the mandate of the church. Thus, our challenge today is to move from church with mission to missional church.[1]

When we started the Tapestry (known to many of us as the Tap), we had a person responsible for Sunday worship, another for the kid's program, yet another for finance, and so on and so on. Inspired by *Missional Church*, I fought against having someone responsible for missions or for outreach. After all, isn't that the primary function and call of the church? Shouldn't all that the church does be considered mission? Rather than seeing mission as just one of our callings as a church, missions must be seen as fundamental, essential, and core of our purpose and action. To this day, we still don't have a missions portfolio or a staff member responsible for missions. Furthermore, we see mission to be the catalyst for worship, and

---

1. Guder, *Missional Church*, 6.

not the other way around. This is summarized well in *Missional Church*: "Above all, the public worship of the mission community always leads to the pivotal act of sending. The community that is called together is the community that is sent. Every occasion of public worship is a sending event."[2]

I first met Darrell at a conference the Centre for Missional Leadership (CML) put together on the subject of missional authority in May of 2018 at St. Andrew's Hall in Vancouver. It was also when I first met all the other editors of this book you are currently reading, and thus, I'm likely the person that has personally known Darrell the shortest of all the contributors. Other than *Missional Church*, I hadn't read anything else from Darrell, but I remember coming home after the first day, and saying to my wife, "This Darrell guy is soooo smart."

Darrell shared many good things at the conference. One of the things he said that I grasped on to and continue to hold is that in Christendom, we have moved from seeing the church as a tabernacle to the church being a temple. For Darrell, the difference between the images of tabernacle and temple are profound. The temple was a permanent building, a center of religious activity housing a cadre of religious professionals. Something akin to what Darrell identifies in *Called to Witness*, "They are built to last forever, to resist change, to maintain their form and activity in as pure a fashion as possible."[3]

The tabernacle, on the other hand, was not permanent. It moved with the people as they followed God's leading into new places. "It was designed and equipped to be mobile, responsive to change, and to provide what the people needed spiritually as they continued their pilgrimage from bondage to the promised land."[4] Not only was the tabernacle temporary, "but at the same time it was the clear sign of God's enduring presence in the midst of the people, pointing to Israel's calling to be used by God for his purposes."[5] Darrell argues that the tabernacle, and not the temple, is closer to the New Testament image of the church. After all, Peter and the disciples called themselves "the followers of the Way," conveying a sense of movement and pilgrimage. Darrell doesn't stop there, advocating that we return to the image of tabernacle, and not temple, as

---

2. Guder, *Missional Church*, 243.
3. Guder, *Be My Witnesses*, 184.
4. Guder, *Be My Witnesses*, 185.
5. Guder, *Be My Witnesses*, 185.

the missional image of church. "At this juncture in time, after centuries of secularization with the accompanying removal of the church from the center of society and public life, we must ask if God has not brought us to a rediscovery of our essential nature as a tabernacle church."[6]

The distinction Darrell posed between these two images of the church as tabernacle and temple deeply resonated with me. When we first planted the Tap, we lived into the image of tabernacle. We didn't own a building. Thus, we met in each other's homes, we met in third spaces such as in the local park and in coffee shops, and at the beach for barbecues and picnics. It also forced us to be nimble and creative. Two of the creative things we did in those early years included doing something called Service Sunday. Not Sunday Service, but Service Sunday. Three times a year, we would find service projects around the city. We did landscaping for a care facility, painted rooms in a senior housing complex, picked apples for the Richmond sharing farm so the food bank would receive fresh produce, and if we couldn't find anything else to do, we picked up litter on the city streets.

The other creative thing we did, and what became one of my favorite Sundays of the year, is that we as a church would do the Terry Fox Run together. Terry Fox is a Canadian hero, who, after losing his right leg to cancer at eighteen years old, decided to run across Canada to raise awareness and money for cancer research. He passed away before finishing his run. Today, to honor Terry and to continue raising funds for cancer research, the Terry Fox Run is an annual event. At a Tap community, we would all walk or run and raise money for cancer research, and then host a giant picnic at the park afterward for all the participants of the Terry Fox Run, regardless of whether they belonged to the Tap or not. I was always very careful with my use of language. We never once *canceled* church. We were still doing church. We weren't tied to a building or a specific worship experience. Thus, in the early years, I felt we lived into this image of a tabernacle, recognizing that God was in the midst of his church and people.

Over time, however, this image of tabernacle has become more and more difficult to maintain. Winston Churchill once wrote, "We shape our buildings, and afterwards our buildings shape us."[7] Three years into the church plant, we eventually came to purchase a building. Suddenly,

---

6. Guder, *Be My Witnesses*, 187.
7. UK Parliament, "Churchill and the Commons Chamber," para. 1.

all our programs and events became located in a specific place and geography. The emphasis shifted from being sent to being gathered. And gradually, the gravity of church programs, church events, worship services in the building began to pull us in. As the Tap continued to grow in size, a missional entropy began to happen as our events, finances, and energy was allocated more and more to the upkeep of the building and to the well-being of our core members, and not the unchurched in our neighborhood.

For me, the words of John in the prologue of his Gospel also resonated deeply with Darrell's distinction between temple and tabernacle. "The Word became flesh and made his dwelling among us. We have seen his glory, the glory of the one and only Son, who came from the Father, full of grace and truth."[8] Jesus came into the world; he became flesh and blood. He became one of us. One of the interesting things is John's choice of words. John could have said, "The Word *lived* among us," or "The Word *came* among us," but instead he used an unusual word translated as *dwelt*. It's the Greek word σκηνόω (*skēnoō*), which literally means "to pitch a tent" or "to tabernacle." Thus, v. 14 can be better translated as: Jesus the Word became flesh and pitched his tent or tabernacled among us. By using this specific word that was used of the tabernacle, John wants us to make the connection. Just as the tabernacle was the place where God dwelt with his people, so in Jesus, God dwells with his people in a new and profound way. Many quote Eugene Peterson's translation of this verse in the Message: "*The Word became flesh and blood, and moved into the neighborhood.*" I love that, Jesus moved into my neighborhood.

What would it really mean for Jesus to move into my neighborhood? What would it mean for Jesus to actually physically live next door to me?

Back in 2018, when I first met Darrell, the Tapestry was in the midst of planting two new churches or campuses. It was certainly a time of discernment. We were in the process of daughtering a new church plant in south Vancouver. At the same time, we were in discussions to merge with another congregation in our denomination in Coquitlam, BC. Thanks to Darrell, I had new language for what and why we were church planting. We were called to be on God's mission. We were going to do so by recovering our identity as a tabernacle—in step to God's presence outside of the walls of our building. Being disciples of Jesus, we wanted to tabernacle into other neighborhoods.

---

8. John 1:14 NIV.

Even though the Tapestry would now certainly resemble a temple, with our two physical church buildings and five worship gatherings over any given weekend, the size and number of church buildings is not the issue. Instead, it is the missional impetus and how a church carries out its incarnational witness. "The issue really is one of theological self-interpretation. A church can be a tabernacle in a Gothic cathedral, and it can be a temple in a remodelled urban store or a tent."[9] My hope is that the Tap would always imagine itself as a tabernacle.

Fast forward from 2018 to 2023, I was fortunate to write a book with Ross Lockhart and Jason Byassee called *Christianity: An Asian Religion in Vancouver*. The premise of the book centers around the changing face of Christianity in Vancouver. We asked Darrell to provide the preface for the book, and in that discussion, we had never once talked about the idea of temple and tabernacle. Even though Darrell never knew how this had profoundly affected me, nevertheless he wrote:

> *God's people are a tabernacle community, who betray their vocation when they focus too much on temples rather than glorying in the tents in which God is present and active. Some have argued that Christendom's problem was (is!) its loss of that sense of tent vocation and its replacement with temples.*[10]

God does seem to know what he is doing.

One more story. A personal one. Back in May of 2018 when I first met Darrell at the Centre for Missional Leadership conference, we all went down to the local university pub for an adult beverage. I had the pleasure to sit with Darrell and his wife Judy. We talked and got to know each other over that hour or so. Among the many topics we discussed, we discovered that we had both been divorced, and a lot of the discussion was on the difficulty of stepparenting, remarriage, and the stigma of divorce among pastors and Christian leaders. Darrell and Judy were lovely, empathetically listening, asking questions, and encouraging. Here was Darrell, professor and dean of academic affairs at renowned Princeton Theological Seminary, the second oldest seminary in the United States (can you say temple?), meeting me where I was. Not only has Darrell written about the need for the church to return to the image of tabernacle, but I have personally experienced how he has sought to live that out in his Christian walk.

---

9. Guder, *Be My Witnesses*, 190.
10. Byassee, Chu, and Lockhart, *Christianity*, viii.

For Reflection

1. Would you say your church/faith community more resembles a tabernacle or a temple? In which ways does it resemble a tabernacle? Or a temple?
2. How has your church building (or meeting space) shaped your life of witness?
3. What creative ways can your church (or you personally) move into the neighborhood?

10

The Missional Garden in a Pluralist City

Konnie Vissers

When I met Dr. Darrell Guder, I was a first year MDiv student at Princeton Theological Seminary, planning to go back to the Guatemala mission field after I graduated. Though I had spent a few scarce months in this context, the people and the place had captured my heart and attention forever. Yet, through Darrell's course in missional theology and practice, my conceptions of mission and missiology changed. Meanwhile, I started dating a man who Darrell had partnered me with for this course. Not sure if it was Darrell's intention, complete chance, or some providential intervention, but we have now been married for a decade, have three children, and are living in urban Canada doing a very different sort of mission than I had ever expected. The missional theology and practice course with Darrell was the first time I had considered that mission is not only a simplified vision of a call to the global South; rather, "mission" is a call for all of us, as the church, to engage in the threefold movement of gathering, "up-building," and sending.[1]

---

1. This concept is rooted in Barth's work and heavily picked up by Darrell Guder.

In some ways being in mission in Guatemala was much easier. I had concrete tasks to do on a daily basis: teach English at the school, take care of babies and toddlers at the orphanage in the evenings, and on my breaks, weed in the orphanage garden and take the compost down to feed to the piglets by hand. I knew my work was necessary and helpful to those around me. I knew that the gospel was being preached on Sundays at the church. I also knew that the oppression of abject poverty had made its mark on each individual who lived at Casa Bernabe Orfanato y Escuela. There was no romanticizing the work, it was brutal hours, no creature comforts, and lonely in every way, yet the meaningfulness of the work was obvious every time I picked up a crying baby, or taught a child a new word, or dished up the morning *atol*[2] for twenty hungry tots.

Yet through prayer, discernment, and largely the teachings of Darrell, I began to recognize that meaningful, obedient work as a believer happens in many contexts. From that one course on missional theology and practice, I ended up taking two more of Darrell's courses, utilizing my learnings in a missional hermeneutics course to lead a Bible study at my field education placement on the Jersey Shore. Then, I eventually took a course on missional initiatives in Europe. This course, more than any other, broadened my understanding of mission further, and allowed me to play with the idea of understanding the task of mission within a pluralist society as one that could simultaneously share the love of Christ and operate with a decolonial ethic. What I mean by this is that mission is not synonymous with missionizing, and certainly not synonymous with conversion. One can share the love of Jesus with others without the purpose of conversion. Rather, by operating out of a love for the "least of these" in our own neighborhoods, backyards, and local scenery, we can enact justice in the world out of our love for Christ, while simultaneously respecting the uniqueness of other traditions.

In one talk Darrell gave he said, "Kingdom planting is our task. But not harvesting."[3] One could be a missionary in the United States, or Canada, or Europe, by being the church—not necessarily in the four white-washed walls of a Puritan-inspired edifice—but around the dinner table, and at the brewery, and even at the park.[4] The missional vocation occurs both in

---

2. *Atol* is a Guatemalan beverage consumed in the morning to replace breakfast. It often consists of maize, corn, wheat, or other grain sweetened with sugar and milk.

3. Guder, "Darrell Guder on Missional Communities."

4. These ideas were inspired by an interview that Dr. Guder had with Stefan Paas around a book we were reading for the course.

conjunction with and unique from the pastoral vocation. While both my husband and I are ordained clergy in the Presbyterian Church in Canada and have served side-by-side in a few congregations, today he enacts his pastoral vocation by leading the ministry of a local church, while I enact my pastoral vocation as I finish my PhD work, write discipleship material for the denomination, and teach at one of our denominational seminaries. Yet, our missional vocations co-occur with our children, neighbors, and friends as we count earthworms and dig in the dirt.

The Missional Garden

After years of serving in a congregation and living out my pastoral vocation in a very traditional sense, I began to consider the influence of Darrell's missional theology which enabled my own missional vocation to take root in a different capacity. In 2019, we moved to Hamilton, Ontario—a sizeable blue-collar city with a history of steel work and a legacy of poverty, food insecurity, and house-lessness. Our next-door neighbors on both sides of our house and our family represent a total of five nations, none of which are indigenous to the land on which we reside. And though the neighborhood looks like a typical middle-class street in any city, scarcely a month goes by without seeing a neighbor carted off in an ambulance from an overdose, or a police car from possession. We also often see neighbors with the familiar food bank boxes, hauling produce into their homes. Though we are afforded many social privileges in Canada, there are no government subsidized school lunch or breakfast programs in Ontario. This lack means that many children in our city go hungry during the day at school. Not-for-profit organizations fill in the gap as best as they can, with organizations like Food 4 Kids[5] providing a meal and a snack over the weekends for kids, and other lunch programs donating snacks to classrooms directly,[6] but the city of Hamilton estimates that almost one in five households are food insecure—meaning simply that they do not have enough money to buy food.[7]

---

5. Food4kidshamilton.ca.

6. Organizations like Tastebuds do this work in Hamilton, Ontario. McCullough, "'We Are in Crisis Mode.'"

7. Ontario Agency for Health Protection and Promotion, "Household Food Insecurity Estimates."

During the pandemic, as I sat in our living room, looking out over our once-busy street, I noticed a person without a house move into a tent in the park across the street, and more and more neighbors with food bank boxes. Though housing prices were driven up by about 100 percent, nobody seemed the richer for it. Everyone just became house poor.

As the visibility of poverty in my neighborhood unfolded over a period of months, I saw a young Muslim girl, who had immigrated as a refugee from Syria to a house on our street. She unloaded a food box from her family car, grabbed something, dashed up to our door, knocked, and left as quickly as she came. There upon the step was a small container of baby puffs, the melting snack that toddlers everywhere adore. Out of their meager sustenance, she had managed to pull a gift for our kid. And thus, an idea was born. Much like parable of the widow's two coins,[8] this child had given graciously out of her little. What if we were all that generous? Surely, food insecurity would no longer exist!

What if we all had food on our tables? And not just cans of syrupy peaches and processed hot dogs—what if we all had access to organic, locally grown produce? If you buy it at the store, you know that organic, locally grown vegetables and fruits carry a hefty price tag in exchange for their being better for our bodies and better for the environment. What if people got to know their neighbors, crossing more than just fences—crossing into one another's lives, crossing boundaries like race, religion, political affiliation? My questioning and dreaming slowly took shape, as did my understanding of my missional vocation.

I remembered working in a collective community garden near Portland, Oregon, during university, where I watered once a week and occasionally weeded, and had all of the produce I needed for my last year of university. The people that came together at that garden had seemingly nothing in common, but practiced the act both out of need and out of a care for the community—donating the remaining food to those who needed it. I remembered the garden in Guatemala at the orphanage. About an acre of tiered land was cultivated to feed the school, the orphanage, and the local community. One week we gave away several hundred pounds of cabbage to fill hungry tummies. I remember gardening with my mom and my grandma as a kid—the sense of wonder I felt as I dug in the dirt with my hands, the taste of fresh dill on a salmon filet, the smell of blackberries after rain.

---

8. Mark 12:41–44 NIV.

For my PhD work in pastoral psychology, I had been studying developmental resilience in children and how spirituality can facilitate resilience and developmental growth, particularly in the face of adversity. I took a one-off course in educational psychology called "Prevention Science," at another college, that detailed beneficial practices of resilience for young people. Gardening consistently came up in studies as promoting resilience at both a community and an individual level—that is, a strength of resolve in the face of trauma and adversity. Out of the reflection I had been doing, and through this course in prevention, I petitioned the city of Hamilton to use an unused piece of land in a local park—and thus began the Children's Garden Collective.

The Children's Garden Collective, which I officially started in 2022, is an organization that seeks to nurture the growth and development of kids through the practice of community-based urban gardening in a city with severe child food security issues. We teach kids how to grow their own food sustainably and provide the food to community families. While I would not go so far as to say that this organization is ecclesial in and of itself, it is certainly a missional community born out of the labors of multiple congregations that are trying to enact the love of God in the city of Hamilton with individuals who most need to experience it.

By July of 2022, the city had donated the land, installed a water outlet off a main, removed the grass to expose dirt, tilled the soil, and added compost to amend it. From there, local neighbors, nurseries, and churches donated money and plants and began volunteering in the Children's Garden. Our incredibly diverse city was reflected in the garden—every kind of tomato and pepper you could imagine, watermelon, zucchini, spaghetti squash, pumpkins, kale, chives, potatoes, perennial flowers, berries and grapes, herbs, beans, and corn. Unlike mono-cropping for profit, any organic gardener will tell you that there is strength in diversity. Onions planted next to tomatoes will ward off pests. Beans will add the necessary nitrogen to the soil for corn to grow and thrive. Dill will keep potato bugs at bay. And like the city and the garden, those who attended the garden to help volunteer, participate in workshops, and eat produce began to take shape as a very diverse population as well. We had people from all over the world volunteering—Britain, Honduras, Ghana, the United States, Nordic regions, Portugal, Syria, the Philippines, and more. We had people of all ages and all abilities, languages, religions, lifestyles, and backgrounds, Catholics, Protestants, agnostics, and Muslims working side by side—thus the missional garden in a pluralist society was planted.

In 2023, we opened our second site in Waterdown, a small borough of Hamilton, on the site of the Presbyterian church where my husband pastors. This garden is smaller in size and serves a different function. At that site, we offered a summer camp that centered on the idea of creation care. It was a Christian camp where we shared the good news of Jesus, but it was open to the community, and only two of the thirty kids who attended camp actually went to our church (my own kids). This summer camp was free, unashamed of our Christian orientation, but also focused on a topic that many people in our city and community care about—climate change and positive practices of environmental justice through sustainable gardening.

In preparation for camp, our volunteer training focused on welcoming in people from very different backgrounds and making them feel safe and loved, rather than on converting as many kids as we could. This approach became all the more important when our Syrian refugee committee chair asked if I had a place for three Muslim young people to volunteer and earn their school hours. I said yes, making sure that they understood that Jesus would be preached during the Bible time, but that their roles would not be dependent on teaching anything religious. We did our best to navigate the complexities of this relationship with care. Their role focused on practical engagement with gardening and activities, but they also sat with children while the gospel story was shared each day, though we did not mandate it. We did not seek to convert our neighbors, but as Darrell so often referenced the words of John Mackay, we had "earned the right to be heard."[9]

In 2024, we again offered a free camp at the church site of the garden and added a six-week class at the city site. Because of the pluralistic nature of our neighborhood, it is somewhat of a dance as to what we can include in these activities from a religious perspective. But, thanks to Darrell, I am not afraid of that dance—the at times awkward moments of showing love across differences in pluralist societies. The gardens at both sites have now become a place for lovingly navigating differences while cultivating love, relationships, and food.

In a guest lecture at Fuller Seminary, Darrell once said the word "missional" was meant to describe the church's purpose "to serve God's healing purpose *for* the world, as God's witnessing people *to* all the world."[10] Thus, a missional community is not so much synonymous with

---

9. This is a common sentiment arising from the work of evangelist and missionary John A. Mackay.

10. Guder, "Darrell Guder on Missional Communities."

an evangelistic community as it is antonymous with a consumer church. A missional community is one oriented outward toward the city, the neighborhood, the world. And the missional garden in which I work, grow, and learn is a place in which I see a dim reflection of the hope we find in Rev 22:1–2:

> Then the angel showed me the river of the water of life, as clear as crystal, flowing from the throne of God and of the Lamb down the middle of the great street of the city. On each side of the river stood the tree of life, bearing twelve crops of fruit, yielding its fruit every month. And the leaves of the tree are for the healing of the nations.[11]

This is what we seek to become, this is the vision of the missional garden— to be bearers of fruit in the city where we live, and to exist for the healing of the nations. As Darrell reminds us, we will not see the harvest, yet we are called to be planters.[12] In a world filled with brokenness and strife, discord and enmity between nations, between tribes, between brothers, we exist to offer the love of Christ known to us for the healing of the nations.

For Reflection

1. Vissers shares how her understanding of mission changed to missional under Darrell Guder's influence. How have you witnessed this change from mission to missional in your own life and ministry, or the lives and ministries of others? What changed and what stayed the same?

2. How can the concept of "kingdom planting" without the expectation of harvesting be applied to your daily interactions and community activities as a disciple of Jesus?

3. How do creation care and our theology of creation as Christians impact our missional witness to a wider, waiting, watching world?

---

11. Rev 22:1–2 NIV.
12. Guder, "Darrell Guder on Missional Communities."

11

"You Are My Witnesses"

Now and New

Renée and James B Notkin

Etched on my (Renée's) mind is a particular Sunday morning in the summer of 2019. Shortly before Union Church's worship gathering was to begin, I recall seeing a familiar figure standing at the church's welcome table. He looked up from writing a name tag and I was greeted by the warm gaze of Darrell Guder. My immediate thought as I exclaimed, "Dr. Guder, welcome!" was, "Oh, no I am preaching this morning in the presence of one of my mentors!" My second thought was, "I want the people of Union to know this articulate, gracious man whose teaching and wisdom helped shape who we are as a worshiping community."

I still hold close to my heart Darrell's words to me at the end of our worship time that morning, that are so in keeping with who he is, "It is encouraging to see that this church is seeking to live out your vocational calling to bear witness in a complicated neighborhood."

In my flood of emotions that morning, I did not realize that Darrell and Judy Guder, now living in downtown Seattle, would become vital to the life of Union Church's pursuit of bearing witness to the lordship of Jesus Christ. We could not have imagined then, that in Darrell's retirement, he would be available to our urban congregation to preach, teach, and guide conversations through the challenges of the pandemic, racial injustice, and the disruptions facing the church today. We did not yet know that Darrell would become a spiritual counselor for our leadership team.

Seventeen years ago, my husband James B and I launched a new worshiping community in the Seattle area with a courageous, faithful, open-minded group of fifteen people who were willing to join us on a journey of exploring these burning questions,

> Who does God desire the church to BE in this world in the 21st century? How do we foster disciples—not church consumers? How can we live as the church—God's called out and sent people in our city—as a blessing?

Between 2001 and 2005 we met with a number of Christians who were disillusioned and saddened by how the consumptive nature of our culture had permeated the church. While struggling with language to describe the problem, we were increasingly aware that the growing emphasis in the North American church on transactional sin management rather than transformative living contributed to a community of exhausted and discouraged believers.

During this time, James B encountered *Missional Church*, edited by Darrell Guder. Already aware of the refreshing teaching of Darrell Guder, through the testimonies of students at Columbia Theological Seminary and Princeton Theological Seminary, I watched him underline, exclaim, and sigh repeatedly as the words on the page resonated with the cries of his heart for the church. The theological insight and equipping of this book echoed, affirmed, and expanded our intuitive understanding of ministry that we both received under the leadership of Bruce Larson and Steve Hayner at University Presbyterian Church in the 1980s.

The growing frustration we were seeing and sensing among many struggling believers and people who were fed up with the church is thoughtfully articulated throughout Guder's writings. It is well summed up by Darrell Guder in an interview with *Presbyterian Mission*, "'The challenge that we're dealing with as we come out of almost 20 centuries of Christendom is the fact that the whole Christian movement in the West, as I think, bought into a compromised and reductionist gospel,' Guder said, 'which focuses on individual salvation and the church as an institution that manages that salvation.'"[1]

---

1. Scherer, "Celebrating Darrell Guder," para. 13.

As we began our journey of launching Union Church Seattle in 2006, the books written and edited by Darrell Guder became constant companions and influenced how we invited people to focus on God's reign. During this time, we met with many people fatigued by megachurch programs, suspicious of pulpit personalities, and confused by mixed messages of scriptural interpretation. I remember one woman, in particular, who was stunned to discover that God "cared about the poor." She had grown up believing that her church involvement was to focus on telling people how to get into heaven while her secular volunteering was to focus on how to make sure people had places to sleep, just trials, and fair employment; the two foci of her life never met. I remember encouraging her in language I was gaining from the collaborative works of Darrell and others about what it means to believe "mission is the result of God's initiative rooted in God's purposes to restore and heal creation,"[2] rather than a revolving door of converting one person after another to Western culturized Christianity. She, along with others sojourning with us, began to express hope in a God who is for the world!

As a new worshiping community, not having a permanent worship space, we gathered in homes, coffee shops, and bars, enthusiastically pondering and discussing God's intention for creation and Jesus' teachings on kingdom living through risky love, radical generosity, gracious care, and hope-filled dialogues of reconciliation. And we rolled up our sleeves to serve together as we asked, "Lord, who do you want your church to be?"

In 2010 we settled into our current home in South Lake Union neighborhood of Seattle—415 Westlake. After exegeting the neighborhood, we decided what was needed most was a third place—a venue and a café where people could work and host gatherings, and where a cross-section of people from low-income housing to Microsoft, Amazon, and PATH could mingle. Through the café and the venue as spaces open to the neighborhood, we connected with people in more authentic conversations and heard stories of indifference and in some cases hostility toward the church—both often rooted in stories of pain and shame because of how the gospel message had been reduced to primarily a personal ticket to heaven or a bully stick from the pulpit shaming people with messages about how bad they were.

Continually guided by Darrell's insight, James B and I were constantly seeking to guide our worshiping community to ask about our

---

2. Guder, *Missional Church*, 4.

identity in Christ in a post-Christian culture and in a church environment swirling with ideas for how to be an emerging church. Darrell's teaching kept us focused on a gospel message of restoration, relationships, and renewal. James B preached in a sermon, influenced by Darrell, soon after moving into 415 Westlake:

> How do we as followers of Christ (aka the church) live into our calling of being ambassadors of reconciliation—people who the Holy Spirit works with and through to woo and draw the world back into relationship with God so that all may thrive? Or to put it simply: what is the church to be like? The church, being authentically the church, is how the people around us have stereotypes shattered, trust built up and hope encountered that creates the context that allows them to trust Jesus and be a part of His movement. This may mean having some of our own understanding of what it is to be the church shattered.[3]

At this time, we were blessed to host Darrell as a speaker. He affirmed our passion to live externally focused, internally alive, and eternally connected as he challenged us to see our identity in Christ as the gathered, equipped, and sent people. He applauded our theological commitment to call our space 415 Westlake instead of Union Church because of our desire to communicate steadfastly that we, God's people, are the church. The building is where we gather to be sent.

As we sought to move from the twentieth-century church's emphasis on programs and buildings to embrace the invitation to be a people who are nimble, open, and creative in our particular setting of Seattle, Darrell's prophetic words helped when he told us that in large urban areas, traditional congregations face particular difficulties. And, he named challenges we were beginning to experience: high land prices, transitory community, lack of defined neighborhood, competing options, and in a stunning prophetic voice that was written twenty years before the Zoom worship of the 2020 pandemic: "The electronic church allows large numbers of people to experience religious servicing without forming any face-to-face relationship with members of a particular community."[4]

These "difficulties" exacerbate the overarching reality in the urban area that would be magnified in 2020 during the pandemic, the growing isolation and loneliness of a post-industrial, tech world. They also

---

3. Notkin, "Ambassadors of Reconciliation."
4. Guder, *Missional Church*, 235.

underscore the need and radicalness of a foundational truth: a missional community is relationally focused. We centered the life of our community upon the three relational priorities shared by Jesus in his upper room discourse: progressively growing relationship with Jesus (remain in me); progressively growing relationship with one another (love one another); progressively growing relationship with the world (sent out). A missional church meets people relationally and asks not only, "Who are you?" but, "Will you join with me in God's restorative engagement of reconciliation?" We watched people begin to thrive as they felt included in the larger vision. People began to embrace a gospel big enough to give their life to. For the next few years, James B and I took advantage of opportunities to hear Darrell speak and to read his writings that refreshed our understanding of Christian witness as "a company of followers of Jesus called by God's Spirit and joined together as God's people in a particular place."[5]

We were committed to be ongoing translators of what we were continually learning as we encouraged the Union community to be Christ-centered and Spirit-attentive. Together we asked how we could guide people to view 415 Westlake, in a "complicated neighborhood" in Seattle, as a redeemed space, given by God, blessed by Jesus, and sustained by the Spirit to be a place of radical hospitality where a new imagination for community for the wider humanity can flourish. How were we to live as Jesus' company of followers who cared about the flourishing of the whole neighborhood and beyond?

Then in 2019, our Union community was given the gift of the Guders moving to Seattle, within walking distance of 415 Westlake. Instead of quoting Darrell and reading from his books, our community of faith began experiencing in-person teaching and provocative conversations with Darrell. In a timely workshop in November 2019, a gathering of twenty-four leaders of our community met in person with Darrell and we wrestled together with what it means to be disciples of Jesus in the twenty-first century. When Darrell spoke of our vocation as witnesses, he created a buzz of conversation as those gathered recalled trauma of street corner evangelists, pressure to reduce the gospel into four laws, and confusion about relevancy of this term.

There was excitement, scratching of heads, wonder, doubt, and perplexity as Darrell emphatically, yet kindly, encouraged us to not forsake

---

5. Guder, *Missional Church*, 233.

the word "witness" but rather to reclaim Christ's definition, as the One who invites: "You shall be my witnesses." Darrell gently charged us to reframe and expand our understanding that to be Jesus' witness involves being a "particular community, empowered by God's Spirit, not only living out the gospel internally but opening up the gospel externally by the way it lives, so that others may see and respond."[6] This initial gathering began our collective journey of exploring with Darrell the vital importance of one of Jesus' favorite words for his witnesses: *allelon*—"one another." As Darrell wrote in an email to David Owens, a congregant of Union:

> One scholarly source I have worked with claims that there are in fact 98 passages in the New Testament where the reflexive pronoun ALLELON ["one another"] occurs. These are the passages which must be taken very seriously when we want to find out how the biblical word actually forms us for our apostolic vocation as witnesses. I would only add that in grappling with these admonitions we always need to remember that they are not statements about works that earn us our salvation. That is a danger with imperatives or admonitions. In the New Testament, they are rooted in God's enabling grace not our spiritual capacities. I like to speak of the allelon imperatives as "obeyable imperatives." They are "obeyable" precisely because they are not rooted in our spiritual abilities but in God's enabling grace. This is all very compatible with the insights you are drawing together from your work on these terms.

Owens's response to Darrell's email reflects how our whole community felt convicted to embrace the *allelon* passages in the challenges of our time when he wrote, "In my reflections, I'm more convinced than ever that the Christian faith and one of the Gospel's core messages is the call for us to respond to God's love and compassion . . . and the call for us to be moving together in our faith journeys . . . to love, honor, uphold, encourage and support one another."

On August 2 and 9, 2020, Darrell preached a two-part sermon series based on Matt 10 (and via Zoom—note his prophetic word) on "Freeing Witness" and "Christian Witness and Sentness."[7] He encouraged us to read the Gospels paying attention to these two words: *Now* and *New*. How powerful to know that God who was, is, and will be, is always

---

6. Guder, *Missional Church*, 247.
7. Guder, "Freeing Witness."

with us in the *now* doing a *new* thing even when we feel we are looking through a mirror dimly! In the midst of all our uncertainty, we are invited to ask what is the *new* thing that God is doing now? This is a vital question as we support one another as sojourners in a world that is unsettled and shaken.

Darrell reminded us that we, as the living people of God, are to always be in a process of inhaling and exhaling. We breathe in the Holy Spirit, the nurturing word, and the life of the gathered community and we breathe out the good news of Christ's presence that we share with the world. From the context of Jesus' teaching in the Gospel of Matthew, Darrell taught us Jesus, God Emmanuel, reveals that our God on high has come near to uncover something radical—God is on the move. God is following through on God's promises to bring restoration to all nations. We are invited to be a part of this journey of healing and hope by going out into the world, out of our comfort with all of who we are—to be a blessing. Equipping, learning disciples take in and absorb what the rabbi says and does, so that they can be the apostles (sent out ones) to be salt and light and live witnessing lives to what God has done, is doing, and will do!

Whether in a more formal teaching time or in a conversation after worship, Darrell has encouraged our Union community, individually and collectively, to ask: Where might Jesus be sending us to stand with him and to be a witness of the living hope, the only hope that can change the world? Where might Jesus be sending us as a community? Both James B and I listened with gratitude that in the *now* of our complex time, God was doing a *new* thing in our community by providing the gift of Darrell Guder in person to guide and encourage people in Seattle—eager to learn, to grow, to discover afresh what Jesus meant when he said, "you are my witnesses." As another congregant who has engaged in one-on-one time with Darrell since they first met in 2019 wrote recently, "Darrell has helped me take another step in realizing our role in the body of Christ. As members of the body, we are all ministers without need of formal ordination. As we walk with one another, carrying one another's burdens, we embody the unity Christ envisioned."

There are many questions before the church today. There are questions about leadership organization, membership, inclusion, equity, worship, justice, and sustainability. The list is long! James B and I discovered that we could bring our questions to Darrell and gain courage to continue forward with Jesus. By doing so, Darrell reminded us again and again of the centrality of Scripture as we focus on the lordship of Jesus Christ. To find our way in the confusing maze of the current church environment that has been deeply scarred by the polarization of our society, Darrell wisely guided us that, "if Christ is Lord of the church, then the church's submission to Christ's rule will guide its structural formation."[8]

After one lively conversation with Darrell, James B provided his summary of our learning by noting that our *new* reality for how to live in the *now* is that we are united in Christ, but people become judgmental in what that is supposed to look like. When we recognize our primary purpose is to bear witness to Christ who is Lord, holding to our differences is not the primary way we do that. What does Christ say is the primary way of bearing witness? Love one another as Christ loves us! When we focus on bearing witness, we disentangle ourselves from a life-sapping domesticated gospel and embrace the expansive gospel of Christ Jesus that takes seriously the command to love one another and remember that God is doing a new thing now.

For Reflection

1. The chapter discusses the shift from a transactional to a transformative approach in the church. How do you see this shift affecting the church's role in society today? What are the benefits and challenges of this transformation?

2. The chapter mentions various challenges faced by the church, including the pandemic, racial injustice, and urban ministry. How can churches today adapt to these challenges while staying true to their mission and values?

3. How did Darrell Guder's presence and mentorship impact the authors and the Union Church community? Reflect on a mentor in your life who has had a similar influence on your personal or professional journey.

---

8. Guder, *Missional Church*, 228.

Missional Theology Shaping Discipleship

12

Lessons from a Theological Hero

Keas Keasler

RENÉ GIRARD COUNSELED THAT we should choose our heroes wisely, for we will inevitably end up seeking what they have sought after. My friend and mentor Darrell Guder is a theological hero of mine. He is someone I have long looked up to and been inspired by. Darrell's life and scholarship are characterized by a desire to walk worthily of the gospel; therefore, I can only hope the Girardian maxim is true and that my work will be marked by this same desire.

    I first encountered Darrell's writing as a senior in college when I read *Missional Church*. Like so many others, I was captivated by the robust vision of a missionary ecclesiology set within the increasing post-Christendom context of North America. I discovered shortly after that *Missional Church* was just the tip of Darrell's iceberg contribution to missional theology. When I decided to attend seminary a few years later, I chose Princeton Theological Seminary in part because Darrell was dean and a professor there, and I enrolled in every course I could that he taught. Our conversations soon extended beyond the classroom, and I eventually became one of his research assistants. During this time, I was also preparing to church plant. So, in addition to being my academic mentor, Darrell also proved to be an invaluable guide for the ecclesial adventure I would soon embark upon.

After I graduated and planted a church, Darrell encouraged me to continue my theological education, believing it would only better serve my work in the pastorate. Eventually I heeded his encouragement, writing a PhD dissertation on missional spiritual formation under his co-supervision. While working on my doctorate, I became (quite unexpectedly) a full-time theology professor. In this role, I have tried, following in the footsteps of my mentor, to view my work in the academy as in service to the church.

There are many valuable lessons I have learned from Darrell over the years, but I will limit myself to sharing three ways his teaching and life have deeply impacted me. I'll begin with when we first met.

Darrell's Doctrine

Within a few weeks of my arrival at seminary and being introduced to Darrell, he invited me for afternoon tea at his residence—a quaint Victorian house on campus predating the Civil War. Having never attended a prestigious school like Princeton, I was still adjusting to my new surroundings and the novel academic climate. Near the end of our conversation, I candidly asked, "How do I guard against this place domesticating me?" Underlying this question was the fear that the ivory-tower ways might seep into my theology—that I would begin approaching God and Christianity as subjects to be studied rather than as a Person to be known and a faith to be lived out. Looking back, I almost blush at the audacity of my question to a distinguished professor I had only just met.

But Darrell was not offended in the least. His response was gracious and conveyed that he not only understood but validated my concern. He shared his own tale of moving to Germany at nineteen to study theology and train for ministry in one of the nation's top universities. His first year there was difficult. Away from family and the church that had long nurtured his faith, he was now immersed in an institution that was given to historical-critical methods for studying Scripture and theology and suspicious of claims based on the subjective experience of the divine. The old joke of substituting "seminary" for "cemetery" in our speech illustrates how some see it as a potential graveyard of faith. The pun may be overplayed and perhaps misguided, as it is often a foil for a certain anti-intellectualism, but there is a reason it exists in the first place.

In that setting, which favored knowing God in only a detached, cool, academic way, Darrell discovered a principle that sustained his faith—a principle that would come to be known as "Darrell's doctrine" in my mind. It was the realization that he was bringing with him into this radically different context all his past experiences of God. Therefore, everything new he might learn and experience would build on, rather than replace, those past encounters with God. This meant the faith he lived out in worship and the knowledge he gained in his studies were not incompatible; both were part of the same journey.

Darrell told me this approach has worked for him throughout his life and in various settings, not just in the academic world. Whenever he faced tough times, for instance, he was buoyed by his personal experiences of God's faithfulness. He reassured me that, as I started my seminary studies, I too would bring all my past experiences of God with me, and they would enrich my time there. Darrell's insight flips the script on "seminary or cemetery," turning seminary instead into a sanctuary.

I do not intend this to be a theological treatise on logical reasoning versus religious experience (à la Schleiermacher), nor to insinuate that our experiences of God are exempt from critical reflection. I just know Darrell's advice helped a young seminarian navigate an academic landscape that is often inhospitable to faith formation, and that his wise counsel remains with me even today.

Missional All the Way Down

Darrell's thinking has also deeply impacted mine, having had a culminating effect upon my theology of the church and of mission. It is why I presently cannot think of mission without also thinking of the local church, just as I cannot think of the church without also thinking of God's mission. Before encountering Darrell's work, I assumed the point of missiology was mainly to study the work of missionaries overseas and throughout history. Growing up in an evangelical church in the American South, whenever our pastor spoke about missions (always with an "s"), it was either to update our congregation on families we supported who were ministering in foreign places, or to take up the annual Lottie Moon missions offering (I just outed my denominational background).

This was perceived as quite different from our church's ministry, which was centered on and intended for, well, our congregation and its members. Thus, our church and mission(s) were unrelated things and never the twain shall meet, at least in my evangelical mind.

Fast forwarding to when I began to read Darrell's writings, I discovered that "mission," according to him, should encompass the character of the church in *all* its congregational life—both its internal communal relations and external activities in the world. This is because the triune God who acts in history is a missionary God, and the church in all times and places exists to participate in this God's ongoing work of redemption, reconciliation, and restoration in the world. I would later learn that Darrell was not, of course, the first to articulate these ideas. Yet it was from him that many of us first learned these core missional ideas, as he played no small part in their becoming theological commonplaces. A chart created by the editors of *Leadership Journal* entitled "Missional Family Tree" places the book *Missional Church* at the base of the tree's trunk with these words: "In the beginning was Guder, and Guder was good. The missional movement can be traced back to this book written by six authors and edited by Darrell Guder."[1]

For me personally, it is hard to overstate the extent to which Darrell's missional thinking has changed the way I read Scripture, approach ministry, and engage theology. Thanks to Darrell, when I now think of missiology the first thing that comes to mind is the local church.

A Hermeneutic of Love

A third lesson I gleaned from Darrell is what might be called a hermeneutic of love. I recall having lunch with him one day while in seminary, discussing a theological topic that was quite divisive on campus at the time. It was not unusual to find students or faculty passionately arguing over this issue, and it had recently reached a boiling point when a student group brought an outside speaker to address the topic. The talk delivered by this speaker—a scholar from another university—was highly polemical and contentious. As Darrell and I discussed our own views on this doctrine, where we each stood and why, he made a passing remark I have never forgotten. He said that whenever I find myself in a heated theological exchange or argument, it is of greater importance that the person

---

1. Editors of *Leadership Journal*, "Defining Missional," 21.

across from me knows that I love them than that I am right. Darrell's words are so etched in my memory that I can still envision the table we were sitting at in the dining hall.

A hermeneutic of love does not mean we disavow critical thinking nor shy away from engaging in serious dialogue of controversial topics. It simply means that, in all our intellectual inquiry and dealings with others, we ought to lead out with love, which is the choice to relate to someone as valuable, especially those who hold positions different from our own. The ability to charitably disagree—an intellectual virtue grossly undervalued and underdeveloped today—should be a hallmark of Christian theological discourse.

As a professor, I grade students on the quality of their arguments and how they support their claims, and as a theologian I will contend for orthodoxy every day of the week. Due in part both to these vocational hats I wear and to my own natural disposition, I can become obsessed with being right. But I imagine God desires I was instead obsessed with being loving, because *being right* isn't included in the fruit of the Spirit. *Love* is. So are *patience*, *kindness*, *goodness*, *faithfulness*, and *gentleness*—but not *being right*. Hence, the apostle Paul's sharp words that we can have all the knowledge in the world, we can be right about everything, but if we have not love, then we are no different than some noisy monkey banging cymbals together.

Returning to Darrell's remark over lunch and what I am calling a hermeneutic of love, I would suggest Darrell does not simply espouse this hermeneutic but models it. He certainly has his theological convictions and holds many of them strongly. His writings evidence this, as do the many lectures he has given in the classroom. Yet he holds and conveys these convictions in a particular way, a way that is gentle, humble, and respectful toward those whom he is in dialogue with. A hermeneutic grounded in love also accounts for Darrell's profound ecumenicism, another gift bestowed upon his readers and students. I am thankful to have learned under a theologian who modeled this hermeneutic, and I can only hope that others will have such teachers.

Honoring His Legacy

Reflecting upon these lessons I have learned from Darrell, I see how right René Girard was: the heroes we choose indeed shape the paths we tread and the goals we pursue. Darrell's indelible mark on my life—through his scholarship, mentorship, and demonstration of a life deeply embedded in the gospel—underscores the transformative power of choosing one's mentors wisely. Inspired by his example, I hope to honor his legacy by contributing to the missional theological discourse and life of the church in a manner that reflects a deep love for God and God's creation. May my work, like Darrell's, be shaped by the desire to walk worthily of the gospel.

For Reflection

1. What does the concept of a "hermeneutic of love" mean to you? How can this approach influence your reading of Scripture and interactions with others in your community?

2. Keas describes how important Darrell Guder was in helping him integrate faith and academic study. How do you balance intellectual or career pursuits with personal faith in your own life? What challenges do you face in this integration?

3. Building on that reflection, note how Darrell Guder's advice helps Keas navigate the challenges of seminary life. Can you recall a time when advice from a mentor helped you through a difficult situation?

13

Shepherding into the Sending Flow of God's Love

Gospel-Centric Relational Witness in the Congregation

KURT HELMCKE

The Relational Witness of a Missional Professor

ONE DAY DURING MY junior year at Whitworth College, I was talking to an acquaintance with whom I had political science and basketball in common. He invited me to attend a regular Sunday evening gathering hosted by Dr. Darrell Guder at his home. I responded to the invitation and became a regular participant in this gathering of students. I recall the thoughtful and refined hospitality that Darrell and his wife Judy offered to us, making us feel honored beyond our deserving. The conversations were about Jesus, theology, and the church. The style of discussion was open to questions, appropriate since the company was mixed in terms of faith commitment. In fact, the person who invited me was not a believer, yet gladly extended the invitation on behalf of the host. For me, the experience in this group was transformative, a watershed moment in my

Christian faith and the beginning of a relationship with a mentor through whom God would guide me into pastoral ministry.

At the time, our campus bookstore featured Darrell's first book, *Be My Witnesses*. I don't know how anyone could miss it, glowing across the shelves in its bright pink cover! Looking back, I recognize that by hosting this gathering of intellectually inclined students who weren't necessarily followers of Jesus, Darrell was simply walking his talk. It was one way Darrell lived out what he wrote about: being the witness, acting as witness, and saying the witness. It was incarnational evangelization, to use a phrase from that first book, and on a Christian college campus, no less!

The witness I experienced in Darrell was relational, mediated through personal connection. It was reminiscent of the life-sharing manner of Jesus as he witnessed to the reign of God among his disciples, a method requiring a relational interest and investment in people. It was centered on the gospel, the message of God taking a relational interest in humanity through Jesus Christ. And it was expressed with the hope of life transformation wherein the one receiving the witness would in turn relate to others as a witness, because "every Christian is to regard herself or himself as a witness, called upon to render witness in the world."[1]

Through Darrell's gospel-centric relational witness, my relationship with Christ deepened and I came to understand myself as a witness to others. Darrell shepherded me into the movement of the *missio Dei*, the mission of God that increasingly emerged as the foundational idea in Darrell's missional theology. It features a flow of sending rooted in the relationship of the Trinity. The Father sends the Son to the world in love, the Father and the Son send the Spirit into the world to empower the witness to this incarnated love, and the Father, Son, and Spirit send the church into the world as an instrument of this divine mission. The church is people, sent to be, do, and say the witness to the gospel, in a way that multiplies witnesses across communities, cultures, and generations. This flow of sending is nothing less than the expression of God's love for the world. The fact that the triune God's sending intersects with our human lives makes the divine mission and our part in it all the more remarkable.

Influenced by Darrell's relational witness for nearly four decades, I've come to see the shepherding task of pastoral ministry as guiding people—both believers and those not yet believing—into the sending flow of God's love: to witness to God's love for them in Christ, to invite them

---

1. Guder, *Be My Witnesses*, 159.

to respond to God's offer of reconciling grace, and to encourage them to become witnesses to the gospel in their own lives that others might also be touched by the love of the triune, sending God. This witness happens through the classic practices of pastoral ministry: guiding the worship life of the congregation, teaching and preaching Scripture, prayerfully caring for those in need, and administratively steering the organization to faithfully fulfill its missional purpose. As I carry out these tasks, I do so in gospel-centric relational witness, witnessing to the love of God in Jesus and calling the congregation to be faithful witnesses of the same.

The Converting Witness of a Missional Pastor

I looked to Darrell as a mentor during the years when I was discerning a call to pastoral ministry, choosing to follow him to study at Louisville Presbyterian Theological Seminary a year after he went there to teach future pastors about evangelism and global mission. At seminary, I came to know Darrell as many other seminary students have—a caring professor who builds authentic relationships with them. Being a friend of Darrell's was an invitation into his network of friendships, which included many followers of Jesus from outside North America. Dr. Guder was a magnet for all who were passionate about the gospel and longing for a more missional ecclesiology than was being offered in the traditional curriculum.

After the customary three-year sojourn in seminary, it was time for me to follow the call of Jesus to shepherd a congregation in pastoral ministry. During the years that followed my ordination, Darrell wrote and collaborated with others in writing the books that became the foundational library of the missional church movement. I read them as soon as they were published, recognizing much from seminary classroom discussions and assignments, now matured and strengthened through collaboration with others in the Gospel and Our Culture Network. Darrell's writing helped me make sense of what I was experiencing in my congregational context. In my first year of pastoral ministry, an elder in the church took issue with my missional approach saying, "as the pastor your job is to run the church." After making as much of an apology for a missional perspective as I could muster in the moment, I realized that there was a very different ecclesiology operating at the grass roots of congregational life. The prevailing opinion was that the ministry should start and end with me. So much for sending; what was a witnessing pastor to do?

In the missiology I learned from Darrell, I knew that there was great value in the congregation, even when misguided (the same can be said of pastors!). I had learned from reading David Bosch that "the local church is the primary agent of mission."[2] Reading Lesslie Newbigin had inspired me to believe that "the only hermeneutic of the gospel is a congregation of men and women who believe it and live by it."[3] I was learning the hard way that the centrality and importance of the congregation in the mission of God does not mean it is naturally predisposed to be faithful to gospel witness or reflect a missional ecclesiology. It was almost as if the congregation itself needed conversion. But how to understand and support this transformation? Enter Darrell's immensely helpful concept of "the continuing conversion of the church," which normalizes the need for the renewal of congregational practices and reminds me of my role as pastor in helping this happen.

In *The Continuing Conversion of the Church*, Darrell wrote that "any local church that wants to be renewed must, therefore, confront its own gospel reductionism."[4] In my pastoral work I have found this to be true. One common gospel-reductive assumption I regularly encounter is that the church is a religious business that employs a person called pastor to manage it and offer religious services. Another is to define mission as one program of the church among many, with little concern for the *missio Dei* that should orient all our activities. Yet another is to assign the highest importance to institutional survival. The congregation and the pastor are in this together, under the influence of larger societal forces: a preoccupation with comfort that preferences a therapeutic chaplaincy model of pastoring; consumerism that seduces congregations to purchase their way into promised success; individualism that prioritizes self over community and calling.

I credit Darrell with helping me see that exegeting the underlying assumptions about the church's mission is a daily exercise, whether conversing with parishioners or reviewing programmatic resources. I have been encouraged by Darrell's reminder that this much-needed conversion at both the heart of the church and along the frontiers of faith is a work of God's Spirit that we cannot manage or program. And yet there

2. Bosch, *Transforming Mission*, 380.
3. Newbigin, *Gospel in a Pluralistic Society*, 227.
4. Guder, *Continuing Conversion of the Church*, 151.

are things I can do and invite others into as an expression of incarnational and relational gospel-centric witness.

Shepherding Through Relationships of Witness

Amid the gospel-reducing pressures in the congregation there is missional hope for the church. The venue for the expression of this hope is the overflowing abundance of relational opportunity in congregational life, among professing disciples yet extending to spiritually seeking participants. The fundamental relationality of a congregation as a community of human interaction makes it a fruitful setting for gospel-centric relational witness. The human institution may be a clay jar, but the treasure within is the Holy Spirit moving among the people as they relate to one another. For the pastor, there is no lack of opportunity for connecting with others in pastoral care, administration, teaching, preaching, and worship leadership.

As a missional pastor, I have found these routine connections to be opportunities for relational witness that serves the congregation's missional renewal and empowers its faithful witness. Influenced by the witness of Darrell Guder, I see my pastoral role as shepherding people into the sending flow of God's love. My orientation as a pastor is to help people experience God's love in Jesus Christ and discover how they might share that love in meaningful ways. The flow of love from the sending God is prevenient to any moment of ministry; my job as pastor is to shepherd people into the flow—both the inflow of receiving God's reconciling love and the outflow of sharing it.

I have this orientation in mind as I study Scripture for a sermon, and as I collaborate with a team in designing the worship service. I take it with me into a hospital room as I visit someone recovering from surgery, and as I train deacons for their ministry of caregiving. I consider it as I encourage an elder or team leader through a tough assignment, and as I moderate the board of elders as they discern God's call and set ministry strategy.

As I carry out this gospel-centric relational witness in my role as pastor, I have discovered two pivotal moves that help me shepherd people into the sending flow of God's love while cultivating the continuing conversion of the church. Both are expressions of spiritual leadership I have learned from Darrell Guder: (1) building an equipping culture rooted in a missional hermeneutic, and (2) emphasizing the importance of Christlike congruence in the way we relate to others.

Building an Equipping Culture Rooted in a Missional Hermeneutic

Practically speaking, if the triune God is sending the church in mission, my pastoral role is primarily one of equipping the church for its God-given vocation as a sent community. The concept of equipping has been foundational for me since Darrell called my attention to Eph 4:11–12 many years ago: "So Christ himself gave the apostles, the prophets, the evangelists, the pastors and teachers, to equip his people for works of service, so that the body of Christ may be built up." As pastor, I consider myself called by Jesus to equip the congregation, and a primary way I do this is by encouraging an equipping culture within the congregation, something very much in line with what Darrell describes as the "equipping community model" of the church.[5]

Shepherding an equipping community is personally fulfilling. I feel deeply blessed to see the people I pastor get into the flow of receiving and sharing the love of God in Christ, stepping into their calling as witnesses. I enjoy opportunities to design learning experiences that help people understand the missional purpose of the church and discover their potential place in it. For my doctoral project I chose to equip people for faithful spiritual leadership in the congregation and global community. I appreciate opportunities to train and encourage people in established ministry vocations such as elder and deacons. Still, there is nothing quite like having the opportunity to equip a person or a team as they explore an apostolic expression, a new venture led by the Holy Spirit, a fresh avenue for faithful witness.

Building an equipping culture has given me the opportunity to mentor others in a missional approach to ministry. A few examples include an elder discerned a missional calling to develop partnerships with public elementary schools in communities of need. This missional move provided hundreds of people with the opportunity to discern their sentness in God's mission, resulting in vacation Bible school being moved from the church to a park adjacent to low-income housing. It also resulted in a community park clean-up project that restored a safe gathering place. Another mentor relationship is with a worship and music director who now shapes worship services and equips musicians through the lens of missional witness. This includes selecting songs that feature fresh lyrical expressions of the gospel and reflect the growing multiethnic diversity

---

5. Guder, *Be My Witnesses*, 105–11.

of the community, along with careful cultivation of the hymn of sending at the conclusion of the service. Finally, a woman called to coordinate memorial services broadened her vision beyond the church membership to offer a compassionate response to people in the community during times of tragic loss. She now equips many people who are sent to offer an authentic witness to the love of Christ. These are just a few examples of people I have equipped who have contributed to Darrell's legacy and will continue for years to come.

This equipping community is supported by my work of bringing a missional hermeneutic to the congregation's engagement with Scripture, primarily through preaching. Scripture is nothing less than the written word of God, but, by its own witness, it is the word of a missionary God, a calling and sending God, a God who works in the world through a witnessing people, a God who creates, loves, redeems, and sustains in relationship. As we engage the sacred story, we keep the mission of God in mind, asking, "what is God up to here, who is God working through, and how might God be calling us/me into this same mission?" Jesus' commissioning words in the biblical gospels speak powerfully to the missionary nature of the church, yet they are a mere appetizer to the missional feast throughout the pages of Scripture.

Emphasizing the Importance of Christlike Congruence in the Way We Relate

From my study with Darrell, I carried with me into pastoral ministry the phrase "mission in Christ's way" from one of Darrell's favorite concise sources of global missiology, *Mission and Evangelism: An Ecumenical Affirmation*.[6] Darrell influenced me to be concerned for Christlike congruence in the church's witness, that the manner of ministry matters and must match the message of the gospel. In Eph 4, the call to equip the saints for ministry is prefaced by a foundational ethical exhortation in v. 1: "live a life worthy of the calling you have received." Darrell sums up the ethics of gospel witness and missional church renewal as he reminds us to "walk worthily." In Scripture this worthy life is revealed to be the fruit of gentle humility and patient love among the believers, demonstrated to an unbelieving yet God-beloved world (e.g., 1 Thess 2:7, 1 Pet 3:15).

---

6. Stromberg, *Mission and Evangelism*. Stromberg, the editor, mentions Darrell with gratitude in the acknowledgments.

One of the discoveries of a missional scriptural hermeneutic is how often teachings on the ethic of love immediately follow calls to missional activity. This is the case with all three New Testament mentions of spiritual gifts in the body of Christ, especially in 1 Cor 12–13. While the proximity of those chapters is easy to recognize, I have grown in my appreciation of the vital connection between the two. After leading people to explore the concept of spiritual gifts as expressions of what God might be calling them to do in God's mission, then noticing how much of a struggle it was for them to express these gifts in ways that reflected the love of Jesus, I realized I had underrepresented the importance of the ethic of love and made changes to the curriculum.

As a pastor, I get a front row, unobstructed view of unworthy walking. The treasure is indeed in clay jars, known to crack, often because other jars crash into them! It's understandable when fallible human beings—inclined to seek first their own will—fail to maintain Christlike congruence. Making use of worship practices such as confession that acknowledge this reality is helpful. Pastors are often in the missionally important position of addressing bad behavior. As leadership is shared and people are ethically equipped, this accountability can be shared throughout the system. Yet I have learned that the worthy walk of a congregation often begins with the pastor. While I began pastoral ministry knowing the importance of ethical congruence in witness, I had yet to face the powerful temptation to force missional change on a congregation. Amid competing visions of the purpose of the church, there are plenty of frustrations to face and moments of impatience to manage. The integrity of the mission demands that I regularly get back into the flow by offering my anxieties and arrogance to the Lord in exchange for his humble, gentle love.

Conclusion

Darrell Guder shepherded me into the sending flow of God's love through gospel-centric relational witness. As a pastor I aim to do this same kind of shepherding. From Darrell I learned that the church is called and empowered to participate in the mission of a sending God. Taking this truth to heart, I've become a pastor who points people to the triune God and equips them to consider their missional calling, a pastor who reinforces that a gospel of love requires a witness that is congruent with the message. My story is far from unique. Darrell's legacy continues through the fruit of his gospel-centric relational witness, thousands of students and friends who are shepherding others into the flow of God's love in Jesus Christ.

For Reflection

1. How has the concept of the *missio Dei*, as taught by Darrell Guder, shaped your view of the church's role in the world and your pastoral responsibilities?

2. Reflect on a specific challenge you faced in your pastoral ministry related to differing ecclesiological views within your congregation. How did you address this challenge, and what did you learn from it?

3. How do you understand and implement the idea of "the continuing conversion of the church" in your current ministry context? What practical steps do you take to foster this ongoing transformation within your congregation?

14

The Gospel We Live

Doug Kelly

It was breakfast in the refectory at Columbia Theological Seminary in Georgia, the Monday after Father's Day 2001 when I first met Darrell Guder. My flight from San Diego arrived late the day before, and I had not found my campus guest room until 2:30 a.m. So, there I was, bleary eyed, trying to absorb some caffeine and oatmeal sitting across from Darrell. I had enrolled in the introductory seminar for the "Gospel and Culture" track in Columbia's doctor of ministry program. All I can remember was Darrell outlining the mountain of work all of us would tackle in the next two weeks. I had expected a leisurely twelve days to read some Lesslie Newbigin. Surprise. Surprise. "Our Doctor of Ministry is serious. We work hard." Those were not his exact words, but that was the message. Darrell Guder has expectations—expectations of himself and his students. We worked hard. *And* we had fun. Theological work is a joyous venture into which you sink your teeth deeply. Darrell gave me that. *And* we did it together, which leads me to another early memory.

It was the next summer at Columbia. Darrell had moved to Princeton Theological Seminary where he became dean the previous autumn, but he was back leading a class in Decatur, Georgia. Toward the end of his first lecture, the president of Columbia popped her head in to say hello, and the two embraced in a hug of impromptu joy. These people at Columbia liked each other! I had noticed it the year before when Darrell and the other two professors, Stan Saunders and Cam Murchison, not only respected each other but enjoyed the company of each other. They had different theologies, but they seemed to thrive in leading the class together. They embodied something, something I would come to realize was instrumental in being *gospel*. And I think this is above all what Darrell has changed for me. The gospel is not just something we speak or do, but something we *live*. *And* that living of gospel is one of the most effective witnesses we have in a world of suspicious nones. That is, when a community embodies the gospel, it preaches.

By reshaping my understanding of the gospel, Darrell has given me better eyes for reading the Scriptures, reading my world, and understanding the church's mission. I have been taken out of an ecclesia-centric view of mission to a God-centered understanding. Indeed, I no longer think of the mission of the church, but rather the mission of God or *missio Dei*. David Bosch puts it succinctly:

> *Mission is not primarily an activity of the church, but an attribute of God. God is a missionary God. Mission is thereby seen as a movement from God to the world: the church is viewed as an instrument for that mission. There is church because there is mission, not vice versa.*[1]

Rather than being dominated by the historic Western paradigm of seeing the church as a sending entity, the church is, in its own location, fundamentally a *sent* entity. What is it sent to do? It is sent to announce the gospel, the good news of the reign of God in Jesus Christ. The church does this announcing in what it says, what it does, and how it lives. It is to this last aspect of gospel announcement that Darrell has had his greatest impact upon my ministry. I no longer see my job as a pastor simply curating a message about Jesus, or even equipping people in doing the gospel of Jesus. We are a church when we *live* Jesus. That is, we witness to our Lord in how we live and breathe church, the way we love, the way we care for each other, the way we welcome, the way we fight, and the way we reconcile. Because Darrell has given better ears for the gospel, I have better eyes for God and God's reign, and in the end, a better vision for the Lord's people. Preaching Jesus doesn't just happen in the pulpit, it

---

1. Bosch, *Transforming Mission*, 390.

happens when the saints gather. I have seen it. Darrell helped me look for it, cultivate it, and celebrate it.

So, what is the *gospel?* This is the question that cried out to me on my first reading twenty years ago of the book edited by Darrell, *Missional Church*. What a rich gift that book was for me, not only giving me a window into Darrell's imaginative frame but introducing me to a whole school of thinkers wrestling with a catalytic theology of the church and its purpose.

The gospel is not just *about* Jesus, but it is the gospel *of* Jesus. It is the gospel Jesus taught and not simply what the church taught about Jesus. To get at this bigger understanding of gospel we must go where the word first appears, and that is in Isaiah. Here the word for "good news" or "good tidings" has to do with the reign of God or the kingdom of God. Isaiah 40 gives us one of our first pictures of the preacher of the gospel, the herald:

> Get you up to a high mountain,
> O Zion, herald of *good tidings*;
> lift up your voice with strength,
> O Jerusalem, herald of *good tidings*,
> lift it up, do not fear;
> say to the cities of Judah,
> "Here is your God!"
> [10] See, the Lord God comes with might,
> and his arm rules for him;
> his reward is with him,
> and his recompense before him.
> [11] He will feed his flock like a shepherd;
> he will gather the lambs in his arms,
> and carry them in his bosom,
> and gently lead the mother sheep.

Again, Isa 52:7:

> How beautiful upon the mountains
> are the feet of the messenger who announces peace,
> who brings *good news*,
> who announces salvation,
> who says to Zion, "Your God reigns."

The good tidings and good news are the announcement that "God is here," and that our "God reigns." When Jesus talks about the good news, this is what he is talking about. It is not fundamentally about himself, but about God's rule. I can never read Mark 1:14–15 without Isaiah in the back of my mind:

> *Jesus came to Galilee, proclaiming the good news of God,* [15] *and saying, "The time is fulfilled, and the kingdom of God has come near; repent, and believe in the good news."*

It is difficult to convey just how much of a Copernican revolution this was for me. Connecting the good news of Jesus with the good news of the reign of God is nothing particularly new, but somehow it had been muddled for me. My gospel, the one imprinted on me, had always been the good news *about* Jesus. It was Paul's gospel.

> God proves his love for us in that while we still were sinners Christ died for us. (Rom 5:8)

> I have been crucified with Christ; [20] and it is no longer I who live, but it is Christ who lives in me. And the life I now live in the flesh I live by faith in the Son of God, who loved me and gave himself for me. (Gal 2:19–20)

The content of the good news is Jesus, particularly his death and resurrection. And it's not as if this is incorrect. Something has happened in Jesus of Nazareth, his life, death and rising; there is this scandal of particularity that I treasure. But that is not all of the gospel. The gospel is larger. (I still remember a lecture Darrell gave in that 2001 seminar talking about the "reification of the gospel," this tendency humans have of reducing the gospel to manageable size. Was I guilty of such reification? Perhaps so. But I was ready to repent.)

Jesus is not just the Message of the gospel; he is also the Messenger. And if that is true, I had to pay attention to what he was messaging. And it's here that those great pictures of the consummated reign of God from Isaiah came to dominate my imagination as I believe they captivated Jesus. What is the kingdom of God like? It's when the "eyes of the blind are opened, and the ears of the deaf unstopped, then the lame shall leap like a deer, and the tongue of the speechless sing for joy" (Isa 35:5–6). It's when the oppressed have good news proclaimed to them and the broken hearted are healed, when the Jubilee year is proclaimed, and when liberty to the captives, and release to the prisoners is announced (Isa 61:1–4). The reign of God is when joy flourishes in the city and "no more shall there be in it an infant that lives but a few days, or an old person who does not live out a lifetime" (Isa 65:20). Is this not the same picture John gives us in the last book of the Bible?

> See, the home of God is among mortals.
> He will dwell with them as their God;
> they will be his peoples,
> and God himself will be with them;
>   he will wipe every tear from their eyes.
> Death will be no more;
> mourning and crying and pain will be no more,
> for the first things have passed away. (Rev 21:3–4)

Darrell, in his lectures, in his books, and in conversations helped me reframe my whole Christology where I could bring together the Message and the Messenger, where the gospel *about* Jesus was not separated from the gospel *of* Jesus.

How then can we be faithful to God's reign in Jesus? First, we are faithful to God's reign when we drop the language of being builders of the kingdom. The New Testament never uses the language of how we "build" the kingdom. God builds it. Jesus talks about entering the kingdom and receiving it. We participate in God's kingdom for sure, but it is as citizens, not builders.[2]

If I am not a builder of the kingdom, how do I participate in it? I witness to it. The task of the church is one of witness. And that witness, to circle back to our concept of "gospel," is to announce. We announce the reign of God in Jesus Christ in our speaking, doing, and embodiment. Before Darrell, the gospel for me was pulpit-centric. Words were the tools of my trade. And occasionally I understood how actions can speak with incredible force. But what had never been at the forefront of my thinking was how we announce Jesus in the way we live in the community of faith. This is of course Jesus' pattern of announcing God's reign. Chapter 4 of *Missional Church* hammers this home.

> The church's own mission must take its cues from the way God's mission unfolded in the sending of Jesus into the world for its salvation. In Jesus' way of carrying out God's mission, we discover that the church is to represent God's reign as its community, its servant, and its messenger.[3]

---

2. "The verbs *to build* and *to extend* are not found in the New Testament's grammar for the reign of God." Guder, *Missional Church*, 93.

3. Guder, *Missional Church*, 102.

Tom Sine speaks of the mission as words of love, deeds of love, and life of love.[4]

Before the church is called to do or saying anything, it is called and sent to be the unique community of those who live under the reign of God.[5]

In chapter 6, Darrell and the author contributors point to what this living under the reign of God looks like: it is an "alternative social order" as the Holy Spirit is creating and sustaining a community as the first fruits of the new creation.[6]

The question is not whether we will be socialized, but what kind of society will have its way with us.[7]

Missional communities representing the Reign of God will be intentional about providing the space, the time, the resources to unlearn old patterns and learn new ways of living that reveal God's transforming healing and power.[8]

As an alternative social reality, the church is called to teach people how to talk, to act, to fight, how to love, how to see the world in a peculiar way—a Christ-like way.[9]

If God is a sending God, and if God has sent Jesus into the world, and if Jesus has sent us into the world, it matters what kind of package we are. As a preacher, I still announce the kingdom with words. The churches I have served have been doers of the kingdom. But I do believe our greatest impact has been on how we live together, embodying gospel. Darrell has given me better eyes as a pastor, always on the lookout for the fingerprints of God in how we love and how this love preaches.

In my second class with Darrell, I remember how he empowered me to take note of embodied gospel moments. In a paper he assigned, I shared about a small group my wife and I were a part of in a Southern California Presbyterian church. One of our small group friends was married to someone who was not a Christian, but he often came

4. Guder, *Missional Church*, 102.
5. Guder, *Missional Church*, 103.
6. Guder, *Missional Church*, 145 and 149.
7. Guder, *Missional Church*, 150.
8. Guder, *Missional Church*, 152.
9. Guder, *Missional Church*, 152.

to our quarterly parties. He always seemed to have a good time, and we enjoyed him immensely. After one of these parties, the wife came to our small group gathering and shared how her husband had had such a great time with all these "Christians" that when he got home that evening, he grabbed hold of his copy of Bertrand Russell's *Why I Am Not a Christian*. He needed reminding of why he was not a Jesus follower. He never came to one of our Bible studies and did not worship with us. But a few years later after many of us had moved geographically, I heard that this man was baptized and soon was leading a major capital campaign at their local Episcopal church. Did he witness something in the joy of his wife's small Christian community? I think so.

Two weeks after writing this paper in Decatur, Georgia, my family and I bumped into Darrell and his wife Judy in the balcony of the sanctuary of Nassau Presbyterian Church in Princeton. I had wanted to hear the guest preacher that day, but what I remember was the joy in Darrell's face about that story in my paper. It was classic Darrell, celebrating glimpses of God's reign in the church and encouraging pastors in their role. He appreciated what I did as a pastor and that galvanized me even more.

The following year I was moderating my congregation's annual meeting. During the financial report, one of our more aggressive members challenged the work of our treasurer, sarcastically labeling it as "voodoo economics." Moderately irritated, the treasurer calmly explained the year end budget numbers. It was not five minutes later before the two, seated near each other, could be seen smiling and joking. Suddenly a guest stood and asked me if he could speak. He proceeded to explain that this was only his second Sunday worshiping with us, but he wanted to affirm that he had never been to a congregational meeting like this where there was so much love among the people. Here was an outsider who was touched not by the preaching, nor our growing mission dollars, but by the alternative social reality he was witness to in our body life together. We knew how to disagree agreeably, how to fight right. We were a foretaste of the kingdom. Later that day, I remember thinking, "Darrell would love this."

In *The Continuing Conversion of the Church*, Darrell has a four-page section, "The Witness of Christian Disagreement." I was reminded of it a year after I arrived at a new call at Bethany Presbyterian Church, Seattle, where I now serve as pastor. It became apparent to me and our governing board that the Holy Spirit was leading us to re-examine the church's exclusion of persons in same-sex relationships from church leadership. Yet, there was an underlying fear of addressing this openly because there was deep disagreement in the congregation. The situation was exacerbated further by an implicit theological assumption that if the Holy Spirit was at work, the body would experience a complete unity, some kind of unanimity. The result was a moderate paralysis based on this fear.

Shaped by Darrell's theology, I saw the situation differently. The Holy Spirit had already blessed Bethany with tools for navigating any storm she faced. Some leaders had this picture of Bethany's history that God has protected it from controversy. Key stories were told of how Bethany had been able to embrace the Seattle Jesus people of the 1960s, participate in the charismatic renewal movement of the 1970s without disruption, and how Bethany had been spared the music and worship wars that plagued so many churches in the 1990s. But the overarching narrative of some of the leaders was wrong. They had imagined that God had protected Bethany from controversy. It was unspoken, but the operational framing was that God had kept Bethany sheltered in the harbor while the storms raged out in the sea. I preached something different: the Holy Spirit had equipped Bethany for the wild waves of these controversies and that her weathering of the various ecclesiastical culture wars of previous decades was proof not that it had remained sheltered in the harbor, but that it was built for any rough sea.

Unsure of where exactly the Holy Spirit was leading us, the leaders were emboldened and invited the congregation into a long discernment process. We were transparent about our differences and committed to loving across them. What strikes me now, looking back years later, was how our Bethany LGBTQI community grew, not because we changed our policies (that would come later) but because we were so transparent about our disagreements and exhibited a love in the midst of them. We were doing church differently than they had experienced before and they could taste it. This was the alternative social reality that Darrell and his colleagues were articulating.

Interestingly and perhaps—dare I say—providentially, when I preached a sermon on the launch of this discernment process, Darrell and Judy were worshiping with Bethany. (I had not seen him in a decade and nearly tackled him as he received communion.) After worship, he was so encouraging of the communal spiritual discernment we were embarking upon and the way we were doing it.

Today, after nearly forty years of ordained ministry, I can join the apostle Paul in declaring that "I am not ashamed of the gospel." But it is more than the gospel *about* Jesus; it includes the gospel *of* Jesus. Because of Darrell and others, I see Jesus as not simply the Message but also the Messenger, who announced God's reign in what he said, did, and embodied. The church, not just me in the pulpit, but the church is invited to do the same. Darrell has helped me to notice that reign of God bubbling up in the churches I have served. And he empowered me get out of the way and on occasion even participate in that proclamation. I am grateful.

For Reflection

1. The pictures from Isaiah captivated Doug's imagination of the kingdom of God. How would you describe the reign of God?
2. How would you describe the difference between announcing the kingdom and embodying the kingdom?
3. In describing his relationship with the gospel, Doug states that the gospel is not only *about* Jesus, but is *of* Jesus. Do you agree with his differentiation? How does that change the way in which you live out the gospel?

15

A Fitting Benediction
Darrell Guder, Teacher, Pastor, and Visionary

CHRIS CURRIE

IN MOST WORSHIP SERVICE liturgies, the last liturgical act is most commonly the benediction. Latin for a "good word," a benediction is a final gospel to pronounce before the assembly disperses. If I were to point to one aspect of my weekly life and work as a pastor that vividly reflects the fingerprints and impact of Darrell Guder, I would point to those benedictions. Oftentimes, benedictions are simply regarded as the denouement, the conclusion, the final curtain to the religious performance each week. The benediction is the only thing keeping the congregation from the rest of their Sunday. The benediction is the signal to the religious audience that they can now return to the secularity of the world having had their dose of religious opiate for the week. Benediction = church is over. Time for lunch. Time to return to the "immanent frame," and the "secular age."

The words and actions in my pastoral work that I find most regularly shaped and inspired by Darrell Guder are those benedictions. Far from offering a nicely tied bow to conclude the congregation's "worship experience," Guder-inspired benedictions impart challenges like "the easy part is over, now the work of church has begun," or "worship is over but church has just started." Darrell Guder teaches me to take seriously the theology of a church of the third article, so much so, that the culmination and fulfillment of Christian community does not occur at the end of the service or even on the building and grounds of the gathered congregation. The gospel is actualized in those moments when the congregation disperses out into the world putting into practice what they have been equipped to do through the Holy Spirit when gathered together. Far from concluding the religious hour of the week, the point of the Guder-inspired benediction is to challenge and encourage the gathered congregation to begin the work of church and to become vocationally apostles, "sent ones."[1] Each week Guder reminds me that I am not called primarily to operate the machinery of the ecclesial institution or serve as chaplain to a congregation's religious affections for one hour of the week, but I am called to equip the gathered congregation to bear witness to Jesus Christ when they leave the assembly.

I have seen Darrell Guder operate deftly in a room full of German translators working their way through Karl Barth's fathomless corpus; I have seen Darrell Guder encourage a student to start a new church from scratch on the streets of Red Bank, New Jersey, drawing from Barth's depiction of the church at work in speech and action; I have seen Darrell Guder introduce Lesslie Newbigin's missional theology in ways that subverts firmly held assumptions and enriches faith; I have seen Darrell Guder serve as an academic dean, team-teach a class with a New Testament colleague, translate Barth from German into English alongside his wife Judy, oversee PhD students breaking new ground, build relationships with students across multiple backgrounds and religious affiliations, and remain connected as a colleague and mentor to people from a wide berth of ecclesial communions. All of this does not just tell you about the many facets of Darrell Guder, but this also serves as a window into his vision of the church and as a theologian of that vibrant, messy, multifaceted, Pentecostal body of Christ in the world. Darrell Guder's own life and faith reflect a nonparochial universal gospel that has something to do with every Christian tradition and communion but that is not contained fully in any particular expression. Darrell Guder's own life and faith reflect an openness and excitement to see the gospel embodied and expressed in multiple ecclesial forms, whether that takes the shape of a staid Calvinist assembly, or a new church development gathered for study and conversation at a coffee shop or skate park. Darrell Guder's own life and faith

---

1. Guder, *Continuing Conversion of the Church*, 207.

are committed to the ministry of equipping, whether that occurs in the theological classroom, the PhD seminar, the collegium of a theological faculty, the fine points of scholarly translation, or in the mission field.

Any good teacher, mentor, and guide does not just impart information, but questions our assumptions, punctures our sacred cows, and prods us to reassess all that we thought we knew, all the while exuding generosity of spirit and collegial friendship. More importantly, Darrell Guder the teacher is not just interested in helping students identify gospel reductions and cultural captivities embedded in the institutional church and elsewhere, but Guder the teacher seeks to explore ways to overcome reductionisms and be better about equipping people for gospel transformation. I remember specifically having my own assumptions rattled in a classroom discussion. Darrell Guder casually commented that there is nothing really sacred about the black pulpit robe in Reformed worship. "Like the Byzantine dress of the medieval church, the black robe was the sixteenth-century dress of the professional judiciary attempting to display impartiality before the Word of God," he remarked, but it was certainly not necessary for the elucidation of the gospel. Not that he was promoting the business suit or the Rick Warren casual line either. He was simply making two points: first was that there is no *one* prioritized cultural norm in which the gospel resides, and that includes liturgical attire. Second, like Karl Barth before him, Guder believed in concrete ways that God can speak through a "pagan or atheist" or proclaimer of the gospel clad in all the *wrong* ecclesial garb, or even one without the requisite credentials.[2]

Far from being an anti–establishment church gadfly, Guder embodies some theological, missiological, and ecclesiological convictions that he believes are integral to any vision of the Christian community formed by the gospel of Jesus Christ. First, there is no normative cultural form or monolithic vessel necessary for the gospel. Second, the gospel is translatable into every culture even if the very same gospel is continually unraveling, re-orienting, transforming, and converting the very people who thought they possessed, understood, and grasped it completely. In the words of Lesslie Newbigin, another theologian and saint of the church Darrell Guder introduced to me, "The word of God is to be spoken in every tongue, but it can never be domesticated in any."[3] Third, no one

---

2. Barth, *Church Dogmatics*, 1/1:55.
3. Newbigin, *Foolishness to the Greeks*, 147.

person or tradition should place themselves as privileged possessors, mediators, or in charge of the gospel of Jesus Christ.

More than a decade ago I had the opportunity to spend time at University of Edinburgh School of Divinity with students pursuing studies in the field of World Christianity first championed by Andrew Walls. Some served in or continued to serve in the mission field. I remember hearing conversations about things like syncretism and educating those in their mission context about the need to disentangle Christianity from the various cultural practices and indigenous religious practices of their host culture. I am not doubting the existence of the need to critique "religious syncretism," or the potential for cultural norms and context to "domesticate the gospel," but what strikes me now is how those conversations uncritically assumed that the Christianity that was taking root in those places in the world somehow entered those mission-receiving cultures absent any cultural baggage and religious syncretism from the originating cultural context. And even more relevant to this hour in North American life, those conversations did not consider that American culture and the North American context were completely susceptible to cultural captivity and our own home-brewed versions of religious syncretism.

Perhaps our recent forays into Christian nationalism and identity ideology (i.e., woke-ism), just to name a couple, are the forms of our own cultural captivity and religious syncretism. A conservative syncretistic faith takes the form of a Christian nationalism that conflates the mission of Jesus Christ with coercively foisting one version of Christianity onto the culture. And at the same time, identity ideology or woke-ism is the syncretistic form that a more progressive secularism takes. Ironically, both movements resist critical engagement, are case studies of gospel reductionism, and are parasitic to the historic claims of the Christian faith and to the theological existence and witness of the Christian community. Both forms of syncretism really care more about shaping the larger society into their version of reality than they care about life together in Christ or participating in Christ's mission in the world. The mission of the church and equipping the church for its sending, both of which I learned from Darrell Guder, must be at the heart of what it means to enter into the world as a Christian community that seeks to participate in the *missio Dei*.

Christian nationalism and woke-ism can be used as epithets thrown around indiscriminately or dismissed entirely. The problem with both is not necessarily with some of their values, but with the ways that each ideology seeks to define and domesticate the Christian faith for other purposes. What I learned from Darrell Guder is that while no culture is off limits to the gospel, no culture or ideology or ecclesial identity is its sole possessor or prioritized defender or national representative. Guder insists that the "confusion of tongues at Babel was not reversed by the creation of one [Christian] tongue," or the creation of one Christian nation or even a monolithic Christian culture, but that the "Holy Spirit made translation into all tongues possible," so that "in the gracious economy of God, the joyful message was intended from the very outset to be infinitely translatable and multicultural," and "conveyed into every language and culture of the world."[4]

No culture is off limits, and no culture has proprietorship over the gospel. Thank you, Darrell Guder. Guder's own student of missiology John Flett puts it even more directly:

> No culture is normative for the expression of the gospel. As an expressly missionary freedom, it is the very opposite of propaganda. This both validates and relativizes particular cultural forms: validates because every culture can communicate the word; relativizes because these forms are directed to serve this message and must recognize that every culture is capable of hearing the word . . . the church is a missionary church, not a cultural church.[5]

The church is a missionary church, not a cultural church, not an ideological church, not a domesticated church, not an American Christian church or a German Christian church or a church of identity politics or a church of cultural reductionisms and syncretism. Now I am putting words in Darrell Guder's mouth. As far as I know, he has not said all these things. Yet I believe in carrying out ministry and trying to serve the gospel and lead in my own particular denominational communion with such an ecclesial worldview and confessional posture, I am embodying a witness, and I am expressing concrete lessons I learned from Darrell Guder. By continually resisting all the -isms and by continually being open to the continuing conversation of the gospel of Jesus Christ, I am actively working for a vision of Christian community that I learned from Darrell Guder.

---

4. Guder, *Continuing Conversation of the Church*, 79.
5. Flett, *Witness of God*, 282–83.

Darrell Guder is the opposite of parochial. He is an ecumenist and someone who is happy to support and encourage one student reading Barth to apply the lessons for a nondenominational church plant in urban New Jersey. At the same time, he is able to support another dyed-in-the-wool Presbyterian student to engage in his missional conversation in the traditional Mainline Protestant context. At the same time, Guder can support yet another student seeking to create an alternative intentional community to embody missional principles in a traditional suburban neighborhood. For Guder, the Holy Spirit does not get hung up on one particular form, one particular ideology, one static cultural norm. Guder believes God is bigger than all that, and over and over again I have seen him teach and live out his belief in a "gospel [that] freely enters all cultures and places all cultures in question."[6] Darrell Guder teaches and practices an openness to the ongoing translation of the gospel into our own context in ways that never let us think we have it secured; Guder challenges us to realize that our culture is not static either and therefore constantly needs to be confronted by the gospel and to be transformed by it, continually, again and again, afresh. In the words of Karl Barth, "one never is a Christian, one can only become one again and again: in the evening of each day somewhat ashamed about one's Christianity of the day just over and in the morning of each new day glad that one may dare to be one all over again . . . the Christian congregation is of one mind in that it consists of real beginners."[7] Darrell Guder does not resist such an approach or regard it as spiritual amnesia, but embraces this task and the opportunity to encounter the world, the culture, the human being before us, afresh in every new moment, with the good news of the gospel.

As a result of his nonparochial yet ecumenical spirit, I would say that Darrell Guder is not a fixed liturgist and not a fervent devotee to the 1662 Book of Common Prayer or even all that energetic about finding unified theological and ecumenical agreement around baptism, Eucharist, or ordained ministry.[8] That said, he strikes me not only as a theologian of the Reformed tradition but as a theologian of the catholic tradition as a whole, but engaging the tradition in his own contextual, missional, and creative way. For instance, I'll have ingrained in me forever Guder's taking the "one, holy, catholic, and apostolic" marks of the

---

6. Guder, *Continuing Conversation of the Church*, 93.

7. Barth, Quotation from 1948, Center for Barth Studies, Princeton Theological Seminary.

8. "Baptism, Eucharist, and Ministry."

Nicene Creed, and reversing their priority to begin with "*apostolos*," and making the case that the whole church of Jesus Christ is sent (*apostolic*) into the world so that the whole (*catholic*) church and world might be embraced by and manifest the holiness (*holy*) of God and become (*one*).

Many years ago, Karl Barth wrote that the sacramental contribution of the Protestant Reformation was the notion that the one sacrament left to us was the gospel, the proclamation of the good tidings of great joy that the world has been redeemed and is being transformed through Jesus Christ. Again, I may be putting words in Darrell Guder's mouth, but I would go so far to say that Guder believes that the one sacrament of the church is our being sent (*apostolos*). The Spirit's actualization of the gospel does not happen in and with certain elements of the supper or merely with what happens at pulpit and font, but the sacramental nature of the church is actualized in its sending. Church happens, church is actualized, we participate in the mission of God, when the equipped community enters the world and offers neighbor and enemy alike an analogy to the incarnation. Church happens when the sent church embraces, embeds, and enters into the crisis, the poverty, the divisive politics, the hurting souls, and the deep need of the world for the sake of the gospel of Jesus Christ. That is the only sacramental nature of the church. That is the church in the power of the Spirit. That is the missional church. That is Darrell Guder.

I must admit, I often find myself hung up and stuck in the *pre*-sent church. The church that prefers warring over purity tests and culture wars. The church that squabbles over who is welcome and who is secondary. The church that obsesses over liturgy or hymn selection or the length of the sermon or the color of the carpet. The church that believes church ends with the benediction. And when I find myself in such circumstances, I give a special helping of thanks to God for Darrell Guder. Guder's vision of the church reminds me that even in such cultural reductions and moments of ecclesial narcissism, I have work to do, a vocation of equipping and sending to put to use, and a community to encourage and to remind of its sent-ness. Guder is not just occupying space in my head critiquing all the obvious gospel reductionisms in which I am surely complicit. First and foremost, his voice is there, but he is there with a word of encouragement. He is there reminding me that I have the opportunity to try and discover anew how God's Spirit is writing its members as Christ's letter to the world in the grit and grind of this particular Christian community.[9] Because of Darrell Guder, it is much more likely that I will embrace such opportunities openly and joyfully. Because of Darrell Guder, it is much more likely that I will not be completely overwhelmed by the demands and trivialities of the pre-sent church. Because of Darrell Guder, when I offer the benediction, I can rest in the assurance that *church* has just begun.

For Reflection

1. If there is no privileged culture for the gospel, as Guder and other missiologists since Newbigin have taught, how do we make sense of the specificity of God's calling to Israel and the church?

2. If Christian nationalism and woke-ism are both cultural capitulations of the gospel, name some others. How can the church be a culture appropriately challenging other cultures, not just receiving downriver from them?

3. How have you seen a church move from being pre-sent into what Currie describes as Guder's one sacrament of sent-ness?

---

9. 2 Cor 3:2–3.

16

The Continuing Conversion of the Church in Our Cultural Moment

Tim Dickau

Every year, our family returned on holiday to the farm in Alberta that I had grown up on, first with Mary, my wife, and then later with our three boys. In this particular year of our visit, we were all brimming with anticipation as we drove a thousand kilometers to reach our destination. The boys could hardly contain their excitement, ready like leopards to bolt from the car and run wild through the trails and open spaces urban children dream of. I looked forward to seeing the familiar places, those buildings, trees, and plants that provided the setting for my childhood memories. When we arrived, however, I was taken aback as we drove into the yard to discover that an old barn had been dismantled, a row of dying trees had been removed, and new structures had emerged. My quick assessment: this was just not the same place I grew up in. I wondered whether my memories were now still as real, or even at risk of being forgotten. The regenerative process that brings new life continued, however, even as I grieved the losses.

In this essay, I want to explore some of the shifts in church life emerging across the landscape of the church's life and mission. More particularly, I want to describe *three shifts* that I believe are crucial for many of the churches we have been working with across Canada and in the Pacific Northwest in a course for church leaders that we offer at the Centre for Missional Leadership. These are three shifts that emerged in our journey as Grandview Church in East Vancouver over the three decades I served as the pastor. These shifts were eagerly anticipated by some congregants while others largely experienced them as loss, leaving them wondering what had happened to their church. Thankfully we stuck together through these shifts, grieving the change and losses, and slowly embracing the ongoing regenerative process by which the Spirit brings new life, just as we learned to do on the family farm.

These three shifts that I will describe are adaptations of the three directions described in the three sections of Darrell Guder's book *The Continuing Conversion of the Church*. Early on in my three-decade long pastorate at Grandview Church in East Vancouver, I read both *Missional Church* and *The Continuing Conversion of the Church*.[1] As editor and author of those two books, Darrell Guder's writing affirmed and refined directions that were emerging in our church. Guder described the topography of the territory that our congregation was shifting toward including recovering a holistic gospel mission, facing a post-Christendom future, and searching for structures that fit our emerging parish community.

Three Shifts at Grandview Church

When I arrived at Grandview Baptist church in 1989, the fifty to sixty people, mostly seniors, who were part of the church felt that they were no longer relevant to the East Vancouver neighborhood near Commercial Drive where our building was situated. Nevertheless, at the urging of our denomination, the joined me in a special yearlong project to help them rediscover the neighborhood, after which I was invited to become the lead pastor of the church at the ripe age of twenty-six. Slowly we began to shift from a Christendom model of church offering religious services to our neighborhood, into a community participating in the fuller mission of God's kingdom come in our neighborhood, working this out in one of the first neighborhoods in Vancouver to clearly embrace a post-Christendom ethos. As one of the early adaptors of Lesslie Newbigin's framing of

---

1. See these two books which are published by Eerdmans in 1998 and 2000 respectively.

the gospel's challenge to (post-)modern Western culture,[2] Guder's writing helped us navigate through this cultural landscape.

A second shift we made emerged from our recognition of how we had reduced the gospel by becoming captive to powers such as individualism, a narrative Guder explicates in the second section of his book. At Grandview, we identified other powers that were narrowing and misshaping our community's efforts to participate in the mission of God such as secularism, consumerism, racism, acceptance of inequality and human-induced climate change.[3] Over time, we sought to resist these powers and be reformed by the gospel through practices of confession, repentance, and creative discernment. These practices eventually spurred us on to form a neighborhood vision, start social enterprises, create housing for homeless and refugee claimants, develop a performing arts group for children and teens, and plant gardens in abandoned parts of our neighborhood.

Thirdly, we started to shift toward new structures arising from this incarnational and kingdom-shaped mission, particularly establishing community homes or moving into houses or apartments in our neighborhood that were in close proximity to each other. These structures facilitated the development of common practices in the *natural rhythm of our lives* and allowed us to form a more porous community that included our neighbors. In these emerging structures, we reflected Guder's admonition to be flexible and discerning with regard to organizational configurations by adopting structures that befit both our cultural context and the emerging shape of our mission. I believe that these three shifts continue to be matchsticks that can fan the flame of meaningful mission for many churches in our secular, post-Christian, North American context. Let me describe these shifts now in more detail.

---

2. See especially Newbigin's two books *Foolishness to the Greeks* and *Gospel in a Pluralist Society*.

3. In my second book, *Forming Christian Communities in a Secular Age*, I describe seven powers misshaping our lives and mission—and then describe our responses to these powers.

Shift One: A Shift from a Christendom Model of Offering Spiritual Services Toward the Forming of an Incarnational Community That Participates in the Fuller Mission of God's Kingdom Come in a Particular Place

When we as a church began moving in this direction in the late 1990s, the landscape was much less explored than it is today. Now, many more churches are attending to this more holistic theological vision and trajectory. For those coming from a more Evangelical background as Grandview was, this shift has involved developing a commitment to and practice of seeking justice for the least as well as a commitment to noticing issues of race and power in building a multicultural, diverse community. For many Mainline churches, this shift has been about recovering a practice of evangelism in their work for social justice and racial equality, in part out of a recognition that a church that does not bear witness to the gospel in deed and word is a generation away from death. In the first section of the book—and for his entire career—Darrell argues for a seamless integration of these elements of the gospel, woven together in the church's call to bear witness and to participate in the healing of the nations.

Connected to the integral witness is another prominent feature of that first section of the book, a feature that I have found to be even more apparent in Darrell's life as I have gotten to know him personally and work alongside him these last five years. That feature is a confidence in the goodness of the triune God of the gospel. Amid all the twists and turns of church in his lifetime, Darrell has consistently articulated and demonstrated a confidence that God's action in Christ through the Spirit to restore and reconcile all the nations is a work that continues amid our post-Christendom context in the West.

If churches are going to make this first shift, it seems to me that we will need to recover the sort of conviction, commitment, and passion for the triune God and God's mission that I have observed in Darrell. This is particularly so given the increasing indifference and suspicion that we have slid into in our age of deconstructing faith. Darrell demonstrates the maturity to carefully weave his way through the sins of the church, especially the colonial history of the church, naming and confessing the wrongs, without wavering in his confidence in God and in God's commitment to fulfill the divine mission to heal all the nations. If we are going to find our way through this period of deconstruction—which can be a needed step toward a more mature faith—*and* if we are going to make the kinds of sacrifices this shift requires, we will need a corresponding trust in and passion for this God. As Sarah Coakley has convincingly argued, such a Trinitarian passion relies on developing a life of prayer wherein the Spirit forms this desire within us.[4] I have been stirred in my own passion for the God of the gospel both through catching glimpses of Darrell's own prayer life and confidence in the triune God, even into his ninth decade of life.

Indeed, like Newbigin, Guder has also sustained a *radical* balance between theological reflection and community formation and action. I describe this balance as *radical* in that the missional church conversation—at least in North America—has tended toward either a theologically abstract or a pragmatic pole. Guder has radically pursued both theologically rich reflection and sustained concrete practices in and with churches. Thus, he avoids some of the pitfalls at either end of this spectrum, whether that be an intramural conversation among theologians at one end or a pragmatic church vision that makes the road simpler than it is and that thins out God's mission by emphasizing numbers and budgets over mission. I long for this radical balance in my own life and ministry—and for the church leaders we are collaborating with—since sustaining this shift calls forth this radical balance.

Shift Two: A Shift from Reducing the Gospel in Captivity to Misshaping Powers Toward Identifying, Repenting of, and Resisting These Forces

In the second section of *The Continuing Conversion of the Church*, Guder describes how the gospel has been reduced from the holistic, global transformational vision impacting persons, communities, and nations to a predominately individualist frame. At Grandview, we began to gather other people—both via conversion and relocation into the neighborhood—who were eager to embrace a much fuller expression of the gospel. As we pursued this wider frame, we became aware of a number of other powers that were misshaping our own lives and the culture around us.

Foremost among these powers were the conditions of secularism so well described by Charles Taylor. In narrating the shifts within Western culture over the last five hundred years, Taylor illuminates how we are

---

4. See Coakley, *God, Sexuality and the Self*. See also Winner, *Danger of Christian Practices*, for a reminder of the temptation to self-deceit in prayer.

so often stuck in an "immanent frame" that ignores or is blind to the transcendent.[5] Harmut Rosa (who studied Taylor for his PhD thesis) describes how life has accelerated to a hectic pace, one where we are pressed hard on every side just to keep up with where we are currently at.[6] William Cavanaugh highlights how consumerism—the desire "for the next thing"—only accentuates our preoccupations.[7] Along with the force of autonomy that makes all communities "liquid" (Bauman),[8] the prospect of collectively tackling core issues facing our world such as the climate crisis, racism, or inequality seems almost beyond the possible.

Yet, when we form communities that inhabit a place and begin to take up practices that reshape our lives and our neighborhoods, those powers seem a little less daunting. This is what we experienced at Grandview. As we formed a community of people in a neighborhood, bound to each other by our common practices in commitment to Christ, and bound to our neighbors in the call to love them, we were empowered to take up new practices of obedience.

One of the initial common practices that shaped us was the common practice of (mutual) hospitality. As we developed a shared life in proximity to one another, we also began to welcome neighbors into that space. In shared homes, apartments, as well as in the church building, we formed a local life with each other and with our neighbors. In a culture of isolation and fragmentation, inhabiting a neighborhood as a community of Christ followers stirs up imagination and courage to respond to the issues our neighbors were facing. As this collective energy grew, we developed a number of initiatives in response to the emerging needs of our neighbors. These initiatives included:

1. A community meal and overnight shelter that later included a drop-in-center.

2. Housing and support for refugee claimants in two houses side-by-side.[9]

3. A social enterprise developer that started with the pottery studio started by two women in the church basement.[10]

---

5. See Taylor, *Secular Age*.
6. See Rosa, *Uncontrollability of the World*.
7. See Cavanaugh, *Being Consumed*.
8. See Bauman, *Liquid Love*.
9. See more about Kinbrace at https://kinbrace.ca/.
10. Recently, Justwork, the name of the overall organization, ended after more than fifteen years of providing employment for people with mental and physical challenges.

4. The eastside story guild, which teaches children and teens artistic skills and stories of the Bible and equips them to present these stories to the public twice yearly.
5. Community houses (both owned and rented) that made room for others and added to the energy around hospitality.

For Grandview, inhabiting a neighborhood as a community with a kingdom vision and corresponding practices such as hospitality, prayer, and justice-seeking led to an expanded missional imagination and courage to take risks. I think that it is typically more difficult to foster this kind of missional imagination and energy when congregations are so spread out over a city with little shared life and daily connection. What if more churches pursued this shift by gathering people in a particular neighborhood, by sharing a life of common practice, and by welcoming their neighbors? Could this shift prompt a spark of the Spirit's new life?

Shift Three: A Shift from Structures Befitting Christendom Toward Structures That Enable Us to Bear Witness to the Gospel's Power and Reality

If congregations make the sort of shifts described above, what will church structures look like? As the culture looks less and less to the church as a site for meeting spiritual longing in our post-Christian culture, what forms or configurations are Christian communities likely to take? In the final section of *The Continuing Conversion of the Church*, Guder emphasizes that faithfulness to God is distinct from loyalty to a particular church structure. When the gospel is translated into a new or changing culture, new forms will emerge that befit that culture.

If more churches do move to collectively inhabit neighborhoods, perhaps more of the gathered life of the church will take place as it did for Grandview in shared homes in proximity to one another. At the height of our shared home experience (before rapid gentrification forced many people to relocate), Grandview had sixteen shared homes in the neighborhood. For some folk, the focus of their common life was within their home and those other neighbors whom they welcomed into it. For others, the shared life emerged with others living near to them. In all cases, these practices of gathering, shared hospitality, and prayer/Scripture engagement were incorporated into more natural rhythms of living. Some examples of this shared life included:

1. A shared meal and practice of examen every second Saturday evening (either in the open courtyard or the community home) among Grandview worshipers in that house and surrounding apartment.
2. Many other weekly shared meals/prayer among and with neighbors.
3. Evening neighborhood prayers in particular homes.
4. A weekly practice of Taizé prayer that was a low-barrier entry point for neighbors.
5. A weekly social justice group catalyzing neighbors and church members into action.
6. Residents installing lockers in their backyards so that homeless friends could have safe storage of their belongings—thereby building trust and friendship between the housed and unhoused.

These more planned interactions were complemented by the spontaneous shared life in one another's porches, yards, and living rooms that emerged out of the situations arising in people's lives. In this deeper shared life, there was not only an enfolding of neighbors beyond the church but a deeper formation that took place through these interactions. Just as monastic orders emerged in ages past as the type of structures needed to foster a renewed mission in a particular place, so perhaps these new monastic type structures can be catalysts of a renewed congregational mission in place today.[11]

In a sense, we were looking for structures that facilitated a more communal life. As Guder articulates, too many of our structures are intended to maintain control of our churches, a sign that deformation has set in.[12] To live into this more communal life that is more porous and open to neighbors requires both a release of certain ways of controlling our lives and a submission to our neighbors, both those part of and beyond the church. Underlying both these moves is an ongoing submission to the power of the Spirit. Indeed, one might argue that it is in submitting to the Spirit in these ways that we are released from the misshaping

---

11. See my ch. 10 in *Forming Christian Communities* for an assessment of these structures that includes opportunities and critique.

12. I.e., sin.

aspects of the powers in our world so that we—and they—may be reconciled to Christ.

Conclusion: The Need for the Continuing Conversion of the Church

The ongoing conversion of the church is a historical reality and necessity. Right now, it seems the conversion required will be more radical if we are going to participate well in the mission of God to restore and fulfill the story of God's unfolding creation. Are we ready to embrace the type of shifts whereby the Spirit regenerates new life out of our crumbing and dying spaces and places?

For Reflection

1. How is your church transitioning from a Christendom model of "offering religious services" to becoming a community that is participating in God's mission? What are a couple of steps that will move you further in this direction?

2. What powers are misshaping your lives—both personally and as a community—and inhibiting this missional way of life? What are a few ways that you can resist these powers and bear witness to God's transforming love?

3. If the gospel calls us to a thicker and more porous shared life with each other (as the church) and with our neighbors, how might you live into this vision? Take the risk of implementing a few of these ideas!

Missional Theology Shaping Vocation

17

When I Preach, I Preach Darrell Guder

Andrea Perrett

WHEN I WAS ASKED to reflect on how Darrell Guder's teaching and writing on missional theology has impacted my own practice in ministry, preaching was not what I initially expected to land on as a topic. While I am grateful to have learned a great many things directly from Darrell, the craft of preaching is not something that I would automatically attribute to his influence. Now, there is no doubt that missional theology has shaped my ministry; much of my work involves equipping *missional* leaders, specifically by leading a *missional* church planting collective, and I work for an organization with the word "missional" in its title. Surely the influence of one of the founders of missional theology would be focused on those obviously missional aspects of my vocation. However, upon reflection, it seems that other aspects of my vocational witness, not just those with the word "missional" in the title, have been influenced by Darrell Guder. It turns out that even my approach to preaching has been shaped by my understanding of incarnational witness.

While I am not a former student of Darrell's like some fellow authors in this book, I was indeed first influenced by him when I was a student. I was finishing up seminary in Vancouver, British Columbia, when Darrell became our senior fellow in residence at the Centre for Missional Leadership. Several times a year he would be on campus to give workshops, guest lecture, provide advice on programs, and preach. During these visits Darrell was generous with his time and wisdom, and he eagerly shared his theology through formal and informal interactions with students. As I transitioned from student to staff with the Centre for Missional Leadership Darrell's influence increased, continuing to inform my practice and ministry. I am grateful for the opportunity of having spent formational time around Darrell, learning from his academic teachings as well as from his example of working out his own vocation of witness in his life and ministry.

Contrary to the title, this essay is not actually about homiletics. Rather, this essay attempts to articulate how my own vocation of witness, including preaching, has been influenced by Darrell's understanding of missional theology. Once in a presidential address at the annual meeting of the American Society of Missiology Guder argued against the need for each theological discipline to include the term "missional" for it to be considered missional.[1] Calling missional a "scaffolding term" he reasoned that the vocation of witness is the "divinely appointed center around which, or telos toward which, all our theological disciplines are to be integrated."[2] In other words, disciplines and practices do not need to be labeled as "missional" in order to be done in a missional way; fundamentally, the way they are approached should be from a missional understanding. I find that this wisdom applies to my own practice of preaching; while I would not label myself as a "missional preacher," it has become apparent that the telos toward which my preaching is directed is ultimately the vocation of incarnational witness. While Darrell has not been my only influence with missional theology, I dare say that it is his particular influence on me that has embedded a "missional" approach so deeply that it has gotten into my bones and become incarnational for me. As my own formation of being a witness continues to be influenced by missional theology, my own preaching has taken on a missional posture.

---

1. Guder, *Called to Witness*, 165–77.
2. Guder, *Called to Witness*, 176.

Being, Doing, Saying the Witness

Now, apologies from this Canadian if I am a bit too on the nose; however, I am going to use one of Darrell's own missional frameworks to help articulate how my own preaching has been missionally shaped. Darrell's parsing of the term "witness" into "being, doing, and saying" witness helps to explain how I am working out my own witness to the gospel through preaching.[3] While there is a clear connection between proclaiming the gospel and "saying the witness," Darrell's expansion of witnessing has also expanded how I think about my witness through preaching. Missional preaching goes beyond the words I say and for me, embodying "doing the witness" and "being the witness" have fundamentally altered my approach to my practice of preaching.

I do not claim to be an expert in preaching; I have much yet to learn. Additionally, I likely do not embody the "being, doing, and saying witness" each time I deliver a sermon; what follows represents what I strive for and, on my better days, achieve. Below is my modest attempt to articulate how I continue to work out my own missional calling, specifically with preaching. This is a brief ode of gratitude for how I have seen my own "being, doing, saying witness" impacted by Darrell's work and life. With that, let's begin this review in the reverse order, starting with the most straightforward, "saying the witness."

Saying the Witness

There is a meme that keeps making its way around the internet, the saying of which you can even buy decorative embroidered versions on Etsy. The picture associated with the meme changes; however, the words remain the same: *"Sometimes I open my mouth, and my mother comes out."* In my twenties, I thought this was hilarious and was aghast at the thought of turning into my mother. These days, I still find it hilarious, but for different reasons. Now as I near middle age and with a child of my own, this meme is comical because of the near-daily occurrence of opening my mouth and having my mother come out. I find I am no longer worried

---

3. Guder has written extensively about the nature of witness and defines the church's mission "to be Christ's witness in the world, being, doing and saying that witness as the continuation of his ministry, incarnating the gospel for the sake of a world for which Christ died." Guder, *Be My Witnesses*, 109.

about turning into my mother and using her words as my own reflect my desire to imitate her a little bit more.

The sentiment of this meme carries through with my preaching. Although, the phrase should more accurately read, *"Sometimes when I open my mouth and preach, Darrell Guder comes out."* When I open my mouth and Darrell Guder comes out, it is done with the utmost honor as he is someone I wish to imitate.

When I preach, I preach Darrell Guder. This is not to say that I am not preaching the gospel of Jesus Christ who incarnates the love of God for the sake of the world. Rather, preaching Darrell Guder recognizes that I have come to adopt certain phrases which originally came out of the mouth (or pencil) of Darrell. I find that when I need to articulate the more nuanced parts of the gospel, or the details of our call to be witnesses, I return time and time again to the words of Darrell.

For me, Darrell has the ability to consistently and clearly state theological truths, with the particular skill of being able to narrow down an abstract theological concept into one or two lines. Of course, like any accomplished academic, he also can expand on the details of these concepts to fill entire books. Yet, if you have had the privilege to speak to Darrell in person, or encountered him online, you will know that he has these clear, but thorough, definitions and explanations of theological concepts ready to go on the tip of his tongue. He can take missional jargon and make it understandable and accessible, with ease. A seminary degree should not be required for people to be able to understand missional theology.

It is this practice of having clear definitions ready to go on the tip of my tongue which I have consciously tried to adopt. It turns out that I have also adopted some of Darrell's own phrases, although shamelessly pillaged is perhaps a more accurate description. This practice has spilled over into my preaching practice, where I regularly employ "Darrell Definitions" to make concepts related to our incarnational witness more accessible. While I have massaged his sayings into my own cadence, and slipped them into my own syntax, I find that it is Darrell's explanations which I turn to when I come across missional jargon in my preaching.

Let me share an example of the first Darrell definition I inadvertently, yet appropriately, adopted, the term "missional." I clearly remember being at an event in 2018 where Darrell was facilitating a theological discussion. As a relatively new pastor I was still trying to wrap my mind around how "missional" looked different in practice, and so I bluntly asked, "But what does being missional mean?" Without missing a beat,

Darrell replied with the emphatic passion he is known for, "missional means joining in with God's reconciling work in the world for the healing of all the nations."[4] Now there is a lot more to "being missional" than this single line contains; however, this definition helped things to click into place for me, and in turn I have adopted it as a go-to definition of missional ever since. I have since integrated this phrase, among others, from Darrell into my own preaching; I open my mouth and allow the words of Darrell to help clearly and concisely define missional, or incarnational, or sent-ness.

For me, adopting these phrases in my preaching is not simply for the fun or filler of adding in "Guder-isms" or using "Darrell Definitions." These phrases go deeper for me because they are trustworthy theological statements; Guder's theology is steeped in Scripture and layered upon the work of the missional giants, including Barth, Newbigin, and Bosch. By "preaching Darrell Guder" it is my hope that I am allowing the echoes of Barth, Newbigin, Bosch, and now Guder to be accessible and absorbed by others. I share these adopted phrases with the intention of passing on the clarity they provided me and to hopefully help make the gospel a little bit more accessible for others.[5]

Doing the Witness

As the name implies, "doing the witness" with regards to preaching is not so much about the words which are proclaimed in the moment but the actions which God, through Scripture and the preacher, is inviting the community to join in with. For me, Darrell's theology of Christian action as witness has helped shaped the goal of my sermons toward missional outcomes and inviting the community to join in with the *missio Dei*, God's mission in the world.

While Darrell is known as a missional theologian, true to his own assertion that all disciplines should be interpreted with respect to the telos of vocational witness, he has taught and written about the missional authority of Scripture and missional hermeneutics.[6] One of the things

---

4. Apologies if I have not quoted Darrell exactly. Darrell expands on a definition along these lines in Guder, *Called to Witness*, 75.

5. This is influenced by Guder's theology for evangelization, that the Spirit enables the good news to be stated understandably. See Guder, *Be My Witnesses*, 137.

6. Guder defines the term of "missional hermeneutic" as referring to the "interpretation of Scriptures in terms of the fundamentally missional vocation of the church of

I am grateful for with Darrell's theological approach is that he never seems satisfied with keeping his teaching in the theoretical, and consistently takes the next step of providing insight into the application of these teaching into real-life situations. In the case of missional hermeneutics Darrell has a basic question to aid with the interpretation of Scripture: "How did this particular text continue the formation of witnessing communities then, and how does it do that today?"[7]

Now to be clear, this question is not one of the "Darrell Definitions" which I am using in the delivery of my sermon. However, I frequently ask myself this question during the preparation of my sermon, sometimes explicitly as I compose and construct, other times implicitly as I review and edit. There is something wonderfully mundane about this question. There is nothing flashy or pithy about these words; however, they help me to direct my focus, or re-direct me when I get too far into the weeds.

Under Darrell's influence with this missional hermeneutic, I have set up a couple of guardrails for how I shape the invitation to action when preaching. First, the practice of asking this question helps me to make sure I am in fact providing an invitation to action for people to take in their own lives and community. Second, as I strive to interpret Scripture with the missional vocation of the church guiding me, this practice helps to remind me of the missional outcomes of such an invitation to action. I am reminded that those to whom I am preaching to are the *apostolate* or those who are sent-out.[8] As the apostolate are sent out into their scattered lives, the proclaiming of the gospel should lead to the apostolate being sent out into the world to "do the witness."

On my better days this question has helped me keep my preaching in service of the building-up and equipping of the community for their own sending back into the world. This helps to remind me that those who I am called to share the word of God with are the same people who God is sending out to continue the witness of the gospel of Jesus Christ in the world.

Jesus Christ." Guder, *Called to Witness*, 90.

7. Guder, *Called to Witness*, 92.

8. Guder, *Called to Witness*, 66.

Being the Witness

While "saying the witness" refers to the actual words and phrases that I have shamelessly pillaged from Darrell when I preach, and the "doing the witness" is employing a missional hermeneutic to invite missional action, "being the witness" is what creates the context in which missional preaching occurs. Neither the saying nor doing really makes sense without being done in service of equipping the community to become witnesses to the gospel. It is no wonder that Darrell starts with "being the witness" in his writings and teachings. Ironically, however, this is the element that has taken me the longest to understand how it has fundamentally shaped me and my preaching.

Darrell has written, "To *be* the witness, the Christian community must *become* the witness."[9] This is a cyclical and repetitive process, done in community, where we are first witnessed to by others, and then become the witnesses for others. While his writing on this subject is helpful, it has been through Darrell's own life and example where this concept has sunk in for me. Darrell lives his own life in a way that he witnesses to the gospel, so that others can become witnesses.

As others have testified, including other authors in this book, Darrell has lived his life in a way that allows him to *be* the witness whether it is through lectures, academic publications, sermons, or personal encounters. Yet for me what stands out is how Darrell himself continues to *become* the witness and continues to be equipped by others. Becoming the witness is not something that is final or stagnant; it is a continual renewal of witnessing the love of Christ through the gospel and continuing to become the witness again and again. Even in his ninth decade of life, I have been privileged to study Scripture alongside Darrell where he has continued to witness anew Christ's love and *become* the witness. By listening and learning from those around him, he continues to be equipped for witness.

It is through Darrell's example that I am learning to shift my preaching from an act of knowledge transfer to my preaching being a part of the process of forming an equipping community. By proclaiming the gospel in a way that helps a gathered group of people *become* the witness, it is helping to equip the community to *be* witnesses to the gospel. Preaching is part of what forms an equipping community which witnesses to Christ's love, not just in what we do or say, but in how we are together.

9. Guder, *Be My Witness*, 105.

Being the witness in all aspects of a community's life, through how we gather, how we interact and treat each other—both among ourselves and with those in the wider community—is part of our missional calling as an equipping community.[10] This is what I strive to have guide my preaching, so that the equipping community becomes the foundation for the doing and saying the witnesses. The influence of Darrell's writing and as a person has converted me to a missional understanding of preaching, which is based on the congregation, or equipping community, being the core strategy for God's mission in the world.

When I preach, I preach Darrell Guder. As I work out my own call of witness, I have found that the missional influence of Darrell on my preaching has gone much deeper than just the words that I say. It is my humble hope that by approaching preaching as part of the formation of the equipping community, by using preaching as an invitation for people to join in with God's work in the world, and by shamelessly adopting the clear and concise words of Darrell so that people understand what exactly we are talking about, then my proclamation of the good news is helping people to take part in the gradual process of the missional conversion of the church.[11] By sharing the common language of "saying the witness," by taking up the action of "doing the witness" and by being formed and re-formed by "being the witness," then we are together working out our collective vocation to be Christ's witnesses in the world.

For Reflection

1. Are there surprising ways which incarnational witness has shown up in your own life and witness? How has "missional" impacted your ministry tasks that you don't automatically associate with missional practices?

2. Proclaiming the gospel doesn't only happen from a pulpit. When you use words to witness to the gospel for others, are there phrases or sayings that you frequently use? Whose words have you used to create your own form of "Darrell Definitions"? Whose words could you use?

---

10. This reflects Guder's teaching on how the "community walks"; see Guder, *Called to Witness*, 135.

11. Guder, *Called to Witness*, 113–14.

3. What spiritual practices do you use to help yourself continue to *become* the witness? Like Darrell has demonstrated throughout his life of studying and engaging with Scripture, what could you do to help yourself and others witness anew Christ's love in the gospels?

18

A Challenge to the Entire Body of Christ

David Jennings

It began with some insider information being whispered to me in the spring of 2013: Darrell Guder had agreed to teach a summer school course in Vancouver and registration would start the following week—*sign up ASAP!* As a practicing lawyer, I had several obligations that demanded my time, and so I had several questions about this lecturer unknown to me and his course topic before making any commitment to a full week of lectures and readings. My informant waved away my questions and simply reiterated the need for me to sign up as soon as possible, as the course would be quickly filled. The school's bullish expectations still underestimated the course's popularity. I was exposed to the scholarship surrounding the missional church and realized that I was like the laborer who had shown up at the ninth or eleventh hour to the vineyard: great work had been done to plant the vineyard and many were already assisting in the harvest. And here in the classroom stood before me one of the original gardeners. And as I soon found out, I had vastly underestimated the impact the course and Professor Guder would have on my life.

I immediately noticed that everyone else in the filled classroom was a member of the clergy. I was the only member of the laity. Soon Darrell Guder upended that judgment—the first of my many such realizations that week. The word "laity" means the entire body of God's people, not only its non-clergy. This was not a mere observational aside but one of the central aspects of Guder's missiology—we are all called to being, doing, and saying witness in faithfulness to Jesus Christ toward the purpose of mission. That insight was only one drop in the tsunami of paradigm-shifting that flooded the room that week.

The course used as its text Guder's seminal book, *The Continuing Conversion of the Church*. In this book I discovered the profound and practical consequences of being called to participate in the work and witness of our Trinitarian God. For Guder, evangelization was not to be reduced to methods and measurable results and the gospel was more than a manageable product to be distributed efficiently. Mission was not another program of the church but is at the very heart of the church and of God. Mission is not so much an activity of the church as it is the *raison d'être* of the church.

At the risk of being reductionistic myself, *The Continuing Conversion of the Church* was written to explain the foundation, challenges, and implications of the church's mission and the need for the church's conversion to understand itself to be essentially *missio*nary by nature. The Trinitarian conception of God's mission, the *missio Dei*, is to be derived from the very nature of God and is a movement from God to the world. It is an outworking of the Father sending ("*missio*") the Son, both of whom in turn sent the Holy Spirit who in turn sends the church to witness to the gospel in the world. This form of evangelization, however, is not centered on our individual and collective efforts, our successes, and our failures, but rather on our participation in the continuing work of God in our world. And that evangelization needs to "be directed both to itself as well as to the world into which it is sent."[1]

For some people (and perhaps all people reading this collection of essays) such an understanding of mission, the church, and a Christian's personal role in that mission has been understood for so long that its expression appears to be unremarkable. But for me in the classroom that week in the summer of 2013, many previous theological, ecclesiological, and soteriological teachings from luminaries such as Barth and the

---

1. Guder, *Continuing Conversion of the Church*, 26.

Torrance brothers aligned like tumblers of a lock that finally answered to the Key (*O Clavis David*). Guder made it plain that being sent into both the church and the world is not the special calling of the clergy or a few believers, but the very purpose of the whole church. If what was occurring was not mission, then for the church it was irrelevant or much worse, a waste of time and resources and focus. So, what was to be done?

In 1982 the World Council of Churches declared "a vital instrument for the fulfilment of the missionary vocation of the church is the local congregation." Guder agreed about the local congregation's vital role, but its acting as an "instrument" should never be viewed as "instrumentalist." As Guder writes, "This is not, however, simply a sociological or organizational necessity. It is essential to the *missio Dei*."[2] The local congregation, or as Guder prefers to refer to it, the missional community, is formed by the Holy Spirit,

> so that the gospel may be incarnated in particular places, to be the witness to Jesus Christ. Any understanding of the Christian church which does not emphasize the concrete and historical reality and the centrality of local and particular communities is docetic: it is not taking with great seriousness God's mission and the incarnation of that mission in Jesus Christ and his church.[3]

In short, "the local congregation is the basic unit of Christian witness if we understand witness incarnationally."[4]

Professor Guder made clear that the local congregation is not merely the collection of individuals. Theologian Bobby Jamieson notes that when considering what constitutes a local church, two or more Christians bumping into each other at the grocery store does not comprise a local church.[5] Instead, as Guder notes, in the New Testament's teaching about

---

2. Guder, *Continuing Conversion of the Church*, 146.

3. Guder, *Continuing Conversion of the Church*, 146.

4. Guder, *Continuing Conversion of the Church*, 148.

5. Jamieson, *Understanding the Lord's Supper*. Jamieson argues that when people come to Christ, they become members of his universal body. They are spiritually one with him. But in order to create a church, people have to come not only to Christ but also to each other. They have to come *together*, and that coming together requires commitment. A local church doesn't automatically spring into existence whenever two or more Christians are in the same town or same room. Otherwise, whenever you bumped into a Christian at the grocery store a new church would emerge, and it would dissolve as soon as you walked down another aisle. A church is more than simply "Christians" in the plural. It's more than the sum of its parts. There has to be something binding people together.

the church, the church has a communal, corporate, and plural character. As important as individual experiences of faith are, the communal character of a congregation does not permit reductionism to an aggregation of individual beliefs.

The constant threat of cultural conformity makes the continuing conversion of every local congregation a spiritual necessity. Such conversion is not an organizational issue but rather "one of fundamental vocation, of calling to God's mission, of being, doing and saying witness in faithfulness to Jesus Christ, the Lord. Our missional challenge is a crisis of faith and spirit."[6] For some, it will be surprising to learn as William Abraham argues that "one of the primary and irreplaceable ingredients in evangelism is the quality of worship in the Christian community."[7] Guder concludes "our worship is therefore the first demonstration before the world of our sentness, as we respond to God's grace in the good news of Jesus Christ."[8]

While a local congregation's worship must be continually converted to express with greater clarity and winsomeness God's grace expressed in the good news of Jesus Christ, more still must be done. The *missio Dei* must infuse all the relationships within the congregation, encourage rigorous biblical learning, and provide courage to its proclamation within the culture. While in the Protestant traditions the "priesthood of all believers" is proclaimed, in practice for many congregations the non-clergy and clergy alike support a clear separation of offices and duties. Some clergy seek a specialness of their calling that leads to a being set apart from the rest of the congregation. Likewise, non-clergy are relieved to hand over their responsibilities as Christians to a few designated individuals. Guder refuses that bifurcation.

In a discussion of Eph 4:7–12 and the work of the apostles, prophets, evangelists, shepherds, and teachers, Guder emphasizes that their "office is not the important thing about them, but rather their calling and gifting to serve the community as students and expositors of the Word."[9] Guder references John Calvin on this point: "we must here remember that

---

6. Guder, *Continuing Conversion of the Church*, 150.

7. Abraham, *Logic of Evangelism*, 168.

8. Guder, *Continuing Conversion of the Church*, 155. That Christian worship often fails to express God's grace is perceptively addressed by Guder and is more fully examined by his fellow Barthian James B. Torrance in his magnificent *Worship, Community and the Triune God of Grace* (1996).

9. Guder, *Continuing Conversion of the Church*, 161.

whatever authority and dignity the Spirit in Scripture accords to either priests or prophets, or apostles, or successors of apostles, it is wholly given not to the [people] personally, but to the ministry to which they have been appointed; or (to speak more briefly) to the Word, whose ministry is entrusted to them."[10]

It is true that the Holy Spirit bestows the gifts to such persons for being apostles, prophets, evangelists, and shepherd-teachers, but those gifted are not only for clergy alone. The purpose of such gifting is to equip all the saints for the work of ministry (Eph 4:12). Two points are emphasized by Darrell Guder in relation to this fivefold gifting. First, "all formally structured offices of the church as mission community are defined in terms of that mission. They are to be understood as functional to the church's mission."[11] Second, "if this five-dimensional ministry of the Word is necessary for the equipping of the church for its mission, then it is immediately clear that no one person can ever do it all."[12] Guder continues, "The concept of the 'solo minister' is foreign to the missionary congregation. . . . The Spirit is not stingy in its gifting of the church for its mission. . . . The conversion of the church will necessarily mean the conversion of many of our concepts and practices of office, ordination, and leadership."[13]

What is a lay person to do once an exceptional teacher makes that truth evident? The lay person must first admit the obvious fact that the gospel places on clergy and non-clergy alike responsibilities as Christians, all of whom are sent forth into the world. However, as noted above, it is easier to identify clergy as having authority and responsibilities while ignoring the obligations placed on lay people and the authority granted to those ministries in which lay people ought to engage. Indeed, I have reluctantly concluded that most lay people (including the writer) often want such an arrangement to avoid the clear call on their time, effort, and focus the gospel makes. It is nothing less than spiritual avoidance, a form of sloth in which we distract ourselves (usually due to fear or self-absorption) from our proper focus on those acts and attitudes to which each one of us is called. To respond appropriately does not imply a "works

---

10. Calvin, *Institutes* 4.8.2.
11. Guder, *Continuing Conversion of the Church*, 161.
12. Guder, *Continuing Conversion of the Church*, 164.
13. Guder, *Continuing Conversion of the Church*, 164.

righteousness" but rather a right ordering of what we lay people do with all the gifts given to us.

It needs to be noted that it is not just or merciful to lay the heavy burden of ministries solely at the feet of those who have taken on the role of clergy while lay people enjoy the fruit. But the tentacles of our consumer culture are many and strong. We come to see church as a product we consume and the clergy as service providers. We determine if the time and money we spend on church matters is sufficiently rewarding for us. Sadly, the message heard from many pulpits only reinforces such an attitude by speaking of why church is good for a person's happiness, prosperity, or some other goal. Once "church" is viewed by clergy and non-clergy as a means to achieve something else that an individual values, the whole message of the gospel is seriously distorted.

A very different temptation can arise as lay people become involved in the *missio* of the church: the presumption of skills and gifts not easily transferable from one's employment or experiences. Businesspeople can quickly assume the church needs to establish a "business plan" with a "return on investment" and "measurables." Lawyers can assume that any gathering needs written procedural structures and legal accountability. Engineers seek observable facts; accountants consider only balances when determining success. The list of these "invasive species" of practices and metaphors is long, and clergy have many examples of lay people trying to run the church as a business, a university, a parliament, an expedition, a household, or any sort of entity other than a church! Lay people need to develop a humility that allows them to submit to the call and requirements of the church rather than impose inappropriate tasks and goals on the bride of Christ. However, once such an acknowledgment is made and habits are developed in response to that reality, God will wondrously use and transform the multitude of gifts known and unknown to lay people as they break free of fear and self-focus to participate in the calling of the church.

Aware of such problems, temptations, and opportunities, I was determined to have Professor Guder's teaching regarding lay people better known within the church. As convenor of the board of St. Andrew's Hall (SAH), the Presbyterian Church in Canada's theological college in Vancouver, I assisted in commencing discussions between the board, management, and Darrell Guder that culminated in the creation of the Centre for Missional Leadership (CML). Board members, almost all of whom were non-clergy, soon came to realize the powerful impact missional theology could have on the church. Some of the most generative discussions I've encountered in the church occurred in the boardroom of SAH in those subsequent years, as we wrestled with the implications and possibilities missional theology presented to us. We were fortunate to have the financial resources to launch new programs and to engage a wide range of people in this effort. The CML has matured greatly in the years that followed its creation. But at its core remains these clear teachings from Darrell Guder: mission is the reason for the church; the local congregation is the epicenter of where mission occurs; clergy and non-clergy alike are gifted for the purpose of mission, and we must "be, do, and say" in accordance with that mission; as the culture changes so too must our structures and our articulation of the gospel to fully incarnate the word of God; and our worship, study, and proclamation should be attractive to our culture, offering a foretaste of Christ's consummated kingdom.

Early on, SAH received a momentous and unexpected gift: the participation of Guder himself. I recall musing aloud in one board meeting, "If people are willing to spend vast amounts of money and travel great distances to play a golf course designed by Tom Doak, Pete Dye, or Donald Ross, why don't we have our theological course designed by Darrell Guder himself?" That innocent question led to a rich and fruitful relationship between Guder and St. Andrew's Hall that transformed our college. Guder's participation in the Centre for Missional Leadership was profoundly important in practical and visionary ways. Darrell provided direction and insight to Ross Lockhart as the director as they built programs, spoke together at conferences across Canada and the USA, as well as helped develop several publications that have blessed the ongoing missional church conversation. But it was also true that his involvement provided a great metaphor to one of his evangelical emphasis—that the message and the messenger need to be one and the same. Christ is both Message and Messenger, and as the missional church strives to be Christlike, it should metaphorically model a similar union.

One final but important note needs to be made. During that transformative week of study with Guder I came to know not only him but also his wife Judy. Over the subsequent years as my relationship with both of them deepened, it was apparent that one of the Holy Spirit's greatest gifts to Darrell was Judy. She too came to know him through a course he taught, and over the decades of their marriage she has provided counsel, translation and editorial advice, inspiration, and much joy. In any collection of essays reflecting on the life and witness of Darrell Guder, there must be indeed a very special mention of this talented and magnificent woman.

As Dr. Guder would emphasize, all of us remain students and expositors of the word. And all of us require continuing conversion by the Holy Spirit to once again make the church into missional communities that reveal the goodness and truth and beauty of Christ's kingdom to all. Darrell Guder has blessed us and encouraged us in that endeavor. May we not fail him or our God.

For Reflection

1. How do we make clear to the church and its various ministries that lay people, and not just clergy, are also sent by God?
2. Tell a story of a lay leader whose missional life has inspired you.
3. Both David Jennings and Darrell Guder have been lifelong learners of theology, open to change and greater maturation. How do we do the same as disciples, "those who learn," from Jesus?

19

A Vision for the Praying Church

Grant Vissers

In my final year of seminary, while I was writing my thesis on prayer and the missional church in a secular age, I sat across a small table from Dr. Darrell Guder. He said something that has stuck with me more than a decade later into congregational ministry: "Look at the way Paul prays for the church." While at the time it was an encouragement to go and do that very thing—study the prayers of Paul and the way they shaped the missional identity of the communities in which he worked—it has also been an echoing challenge to the way I think about my own life and ministry in the local church. Darrell's own life and influence on mine is not only as a theologian and pastor, but as one who, himself, is deeply rooted in prayer. As a follower of Jesus, a husband, a father, and a pastor, prayer has become crucial to the way I live and lead. While that may seem like a foregone conclusion, as one who is deeply driven to distraction, it has been a habit that has not come easily. It has, however, become deeply integrated into my life because of people like Darrell who not only spoke about prayer but who demonstrated it lived out daily.

The church must pray. Prayer is, to borrow Karl Barth's language, "absolutely indispensable"[1] to the identity and vocation of the church. To cease in its praying, is to cease being the church of Jesus Christ in and for the world. What Paul demonstrates in his letters is how to lead and give vision to a community *through* prayer. For the church to pray, the pastor must pray. Similarly, I wonder, for the pastor to cease prayer is for the pastor to cease ministering to God and people. "Pray without ceasing,"[2] challenges Paul—to the follower of Jesus and to the community alike.

Throughout his letters, Paul gives voice to the praying pastor, and, in doing so, the praying church. When you catalog Paul's prayers for the early church communities, many of which he founded, you see the heart of a pastor that is driven to help equip communities of faith live into the realities of the kingdom of God—grace, peace, love, unity, witness, calling, proclamation, and prayer. In Ephesians and Philippians, Paul gives a picture of the missional church which is formed by Jesus for the sake of this coming kingdom. In Ephesians, while not a prayer, Paul declares his hope for the church as he urges the people to "live a life worthy of the calling to which you have been called."[3] In his prayer for the church in Philippi, Paul rejoices because followers of Jesus had embraced being "partners in the gospel, from the first day until now."[4] Given this picture of the missional community—the church is the community of those who are "called out," to give witness to the coming kingdom of God. And more than that, *if* they are ones who are called to become partners (coworkers) in the kingdom's very coming, *then* the church needs to be one that "prays without ceasing." Again, I hear Darrell's words, spoken, but also written concretely in *Missional Church*, "Prayer is not about getting

---

1. Barth, *Church Dogmatics*, 4/3.2:882 (note: from this point on I will be footnoting the *Church Dogmatics* simply as "*CD*" with section and page numbers). Here Barth fleshes out the idea that the prayer is an indispensable work of the church as the gathered community of Jesus. He writes: "The community works but it also prays. More precisely, it prays as it works. And in praying, it works. Prayer is not just an occasional breathing of the soul, nor is it merely an individual elevation of the heart. It is a movement in which Christians jointly and persistently engage. It is absolutely indispensable in the accomplishment of the action required of the community. It cannot be separated from this action. Prayer is a basic element in the whole action of the whole community. 'Pray without ceasing' (1 Thess 5:17). Hence prayer—we are reminded of the first-person plural in the Lord's Prayer—is a work of the community."

2. 1 Thess 5:17.

3. Eph 4:1.

4. Phil 1:3–6.

what we want—the fulfillment of our will; it is about learning what God wants—the bending of our will to God's will."[5] Through the practice of prayer, we learn to pray without ceasing the prayer that Jesus taught his disciples, "Your kingdom come, your will be done, on earth as it is in heaven,"[6] and we learn to work according to that kingdom's coming.

The question I keep returning to in congregational ministry is firstly this: "What might the church look like if we continue to be and become ones who pray the missional church into existence—in our lifetime and in our context?" In his lecture fragments, Karl Barth writes, "Christians pray to God that he will cause his righteousness to appear and dwell on a new earth under a new heaven. Meanwhile *they act* in accordance with their prayer as people who are responsible for the rule of human righteousness."[7] Prayer is the mechanism that allows our minds, hearts, souls, and lives to be drawn into the vision that Jesus has for his church. It's a question that has no singular answer because it opens us to the reality that God will continue to inspire faithful followers to creatively engage the gospel in their communities. But equally, I also wonder how we can practically foster a spirit of prayer and the discipline of prayer *so that* we allow ourselves to be opened to the vision God has for his church. I haven't yet learned how to convince God to speak to me in any given time or space (I wish I could), but I am convinced that we can position ourselves, in a disciplined way, repeatedly, so that we are ready when God speaks.

Here together, Guder, Paul, and Barth offer us a way forward. In "The Community for the World" Barth writes, "[The church] is the community of Jesus Christ and has its basis of its being and nature in Him. He calls, gathers and upbuilds it."[8] To the church's calling, gathering, and upbuilding, Darrell emphasizes the church's sending as its third movement when he writes, "[Just as] we have learned to speak of God as a missionary God . . . we have learned to understand the church as sent people."[9] If the church finds its existence in this trifold movement—its gathering, its equipping, and its sending—prayer serves the very practical job of continually calling the church back to these movements. We will

---

5. Guder, *Missional Church*, 157–58.
6. Matt 6:10.
7. Barth, *CD* 4/4:205, lecture fragments.
8. Barth, *CD* 4/3.2:763.
9. Guder, *Missional Church*, 4.

explore these three movements of prayer below: Jesus calls his church to be gathered, equipped, and sent into the world.

The Church Is Gathered in Prayer

> For what thanksgiving can we return to God for you, for all the joy that we feel for your sake before our God, as we pray most earnestly night and day that we may see you face to face.
> —1 Thess 3:9–10 (ESV)

Prayer gathers the community. Almost exactly four years ago from the time I am writing these words, on March 15, 2020, our church hosted its first fully online worship service in its then 167 years of existence. This same line would be true for countless churches across North America and the world. In the beginning stages of the COVID-19 pandemic, pastors and leaders scrambled to provide a mechanism for churches to continue worshiping while realizing that physical gatherings were not possible in the interim. As the pandemic continued, as did restrictions on physical gatherings, our teams became more proficient at recording and streaming live worship. We raised the financial resources required to purchase cameras and increase the quality of Sunday's "productions." I am proud of our teams of volunteers, our staff, and our church for leaning into that season. However, as I look back, the most authentic gatherings weren't found on YouTube or in the reproduction of a live worship service that could be consumed when it became convenient. The most authentic gatherings were the ones where we committed ourselves to prayer. There were times when that meant gathering digitally, and there were times when it meant meeting in person. There were large groups who met to pray and there were faithful followers of Jesus who picked up the phone to pray with just one other person.

Prayer was the practice that gathered the community, and, in many ways, it was how we remained faithful in our gathering as the community when so many other ministry options were limited. In prayer, the Holy Spirit gathered us together to be and to become the community of Jesus Christ present for one another in a season of great loneliness, isolation, and uncertainty.

In one of his earliest letters, Paul writes to the church in Thessalonica a prayer that helps name the felt human need for community. "For what thanksgiving can we return to God for you, for all the joy that we feel for your sake before our God, as we pray most earnestly night and day that we may see you face to face and supply what is lacking in your faith?"[10] Paul's prayers demonstrate the need for human connection and the call that is placed on the Christian church to be gathered together. While we no longer face the same challenges as we once did, challenges still abound in the life of the church as does great joy and celebration. The Holy Spirit still gathers us in intentional prayer as we continue to be and become the community of Jesus in our time and in our context. While this is not a prescription for every church, for us it looks like routine, weekly prayer every Sunday morning before worship. It looks like faithful followers gathering each week in each other's homes for prayer. It looks like weekly staff gatherings with prayer. It looks like a small upper room in our building, dedicated for prayer. Frequently visited, but never the center of attention. To be honest, it usually isn't glamorous; it looks like boring and even mundane gatherings to sit and be still, to listen and to pray together. And yet, we know that it is absolutely the discipline that we are called to practice with great care and passion, with excitement and with certainty that is in no way mundane. It is where we glimpse visions of the kingdom of heaven on earth and where we catch God's vision for us on earth just like it is in heaven. Prayer gathers the community.

The Church Is Equipped by Prayer

> And so, from the day we heard, we have not ceased to pray for you, asking that you may be filled with the knowledge of his will in all spiritual wisdom and understanding, so as to walk in a manner worthy of the Lord, fully pleasing to him: bearing fruit in every good work and increasing in the knowledge of God.
> —Col 1:3–14 (ESV)

Prayer equips the community. One of my favorite rooms at the camp where I worked for years was called "The Tripping Room." Likely not named so because of the rickety stairs that I always fell down coming out of the small room, but because it held every piece of equipment imaginable that one would need while leading a canoe trip. It was the room that we visited every week to refill our fuel and repair or exchange defective cooking stoves. There were replacement parts for tents and supplies to patch holes in sides of canoes, something that seemed to happen often.

---

10. 1 Thess 3:9.

It was the room that equipped us for whatever white water, lake-hopping (mis)adventure that was next.

Equipping of any sort always serves a purpose or is directed toward an end—we are equipped for a reason. Darrell's influence on my theology and ministry has been to always see that purpose and end as the vocation of Christian witness. If, as Darrell writes, "we have learned to understand the church as sent people,"[11] we must also learn to understand prayer as a means through which the Spirit equips the church for its sending into the world. The principal way the church needs to be equipped is in the continual alignment of our wills and hearts to God's. How do we intentionally work to ensure that we aren't simply chasing the personal, individual benefits of what it means to be a Christian? How do we maintain a vision of God's kingdom and not our own kingdoms? We pray. Above all else, prayer is the action that the church participates in which grounds it in Jesus' vision of the kingdom, equips it for witness, and commissions it to be sent out into the world as faithful witnesses to the gospel.

Paul tells the Colossian community that he has "not ceased to pray for you, asking that you may be filled with the knowledge of his will in all spiritual wisdom and understanding, so as to walk in a manner worthy of the Lord, fully pleasing to him: bearing fruit in every good work and increasing in the knowledge of God."[12] His prayer was for a community, and it is important to begin by reminding us that it was for a community—together. Paul's prayer is, and ours needs to be, corporate. As we are gathered, and equipped, as we pray, we are reminded that our calling is toward community. Paul's hope is that, together, the Colossians would be filled with the knowledge of God's will, for spiritual wisdom and for understanding, the result being a community that bears good fruit. The result of knowledge, wisdom, and understanding is fruit. Equally, the result of Paul's prayer is that same fruit. Through prayer, Paul encourages the equipping of the community for the work of the kingdom and perhaps gives them a vision for how they might pray together—that they would be equipped to do the work with which they have been tasked. Similarly, through prayer, God speaks to and equips our churches—our communities. Prayer encourages and challenges; prayer convicts and transforms; prayer reforms and reminds us of God's will. The church is equipped for

---

11. Guder, *Missional Church*, 4.
12. Col 1:9–10.

its task—its mission in the world—through prayer. We are reminded that it is a task that we must persistently engage together.

The Church Is Sent Through Prayer

> May the God of endurance and encouragement grant you to live in such harmony with one another, in accord with Christ Jesus, ⁶ that together you may with one voice glorify the God and Father of our Lord Jesus Christ.
> —Rom 15:5–6 (ESV)

Prayer sends the community. I am reminded of a friend of mine, and pastor, who always said that the benediction is the most important part of Christian worship because it is when the worship is taken into the world with a purpose. The church does not exist in and for itself; it exists for the world. In *Here and Now* Barth writes, "The essence of the church is the event in which the community is a light shining also in the world."[13] In his book *Be My Witnesses*, Darrell frames the vocation of the Christian community with these words, "The church exists because God has called it forth. Its mission is to be, to do, and to say the witness to God's saving actions and purposes [in the world]."[14] As we are gathered, and equipped, prayer serves to remind us that the church does not exist for itself, but for the world. In Jesus' prayer for the disciples and all who would believe, he prays "that they may become perfectly one, *so that the world may know* that you sent me and loved them even as you loved me."[15] The outcome of Jesus' prayer is a world that knows God and the love that is shared in and through the life of Jesus. Our prayer, too, reminds us of this future vision, where people know the love of God in and through the person of Jesus and where we are faithful witnesses and coworkers in the kingdom. The road of Christian witness in Canada in 2024 is rocky, and yet somehow the ground is still fertile. Certainly, Jesus' words ring true, "The harvest is plentiful" (Matt 9:37). As I think through what it means to be sent through prayer, I am reminded of John Mackay's words when writing and speaking about mission work in foreign culture; he said communities must "earn the right to be heard through particular service that met

---

13. Barth, *Here and Now*, 81.
14. Guder, *Be My Witnesses*, 153.
15. John 17:21.

specific needs within the receiving culture."[16] Certainly, this rings true when it comes to evangelism on secular, post-Christian Canadian soil. Communities of faith must allow God to direct our sending and trust in the Spirit's leading. In *The Jesus Way: A Conversation on the Ways That Jesus Is the Way*, Eugene Peterson writes,

> The way of Jesus cannot be imposed or mapped—it requires an active participation in following Jesus as He leads us through sometimes strange and unfamiliar territory, in circumstances that become clear only in the hesitations and questionings, in the pauses and reflections where we engage in prayerful conversation with one another and with Him.[17]

The hope that the Christian community is given through prayer is that our work as witnesses in the world is constantly directed by the Spirit's leading—provided we listen.

Conclusion

The longer I am alive, the more I appreciate these influences that have driven me toward practices of prayer that shape and form my life as a follower of Jesus. It took having three children to really and truly appreciate the rhythm of an early morning routine. It also took having three children to finally put one into *practice*. There are days where I succeed and days where I fail—sometimes miserably. But there is comfort in the discipline of regular morning prayer. Similarly, in the way we live our collective life as the church, there is something life-giving about the routine and disciplined practice of prayer. In our gathering, equipping, and sending, in our prayer, we are reminded of who we are and whose we are—dearly beloved, called to walk worthily and live brightly as witnesses in the world. The very first class I sat in at seminary was not a class with Darrell, but the very first class where a professor began with prayer *was* a class with Darrell—his life speaking to this routine and disciplined movement: to be gathered in prayer, equipped by prayer, and sent out through prayer.

---

16. This quote is attributed to John A. Mackay. I came to Mackay through lectures and conversations with Darrell Guder. This phrase was particularly impactful during early lectures at seminary.

17. Peterson, *Jesus Way*, 18.

For Reflection

1. Is there a missional practice, like prayer, that you have struggled to include in your discipleship routine? How has someone encouraged you to continue to engage with the practice? What difference has it made for you?

2. When we observe disciples engage with missional practices like prayer, we can be encouraged to include those practices in our own spiritual formation. How have you been encouraged by disciples? How have you or could you encourage others?

3. How have your prayer practices changes over time? What has worked well over the years or is something that has never seemed to be a fit? What practice do you wish you could add or abandon?

20

Darrell Who?

COREY SCHLOSSER-HALL

"Who?" I asked. "Dr. Darrell Guder," my colleague Rev. Fred Garry replied. "You know, the one who wrote *Missional Church* with some of those other writers." "Never heard of him," I shot back. "Why would you want to invite him?" It was 2002 in Seattle. Fred was the chair of the Seattle Presbytery's mission committee. We were on our way to a dim sum lunch in late summer in sunny (yeah, you heard that right . . . sunny) south Seattle when he described for me what he wanted to do. "I want to bring people to the presbytery who will shake up our understanding of church and what it means to offer servant leadership today," Fred matter-of-factly shared.

I thought to myself, sounds like a great idea, but really . . . a guy named Darrell . . . and my other brother Darrell?

Darrell the Mind-Flipper

I had begun serving as the communications director in Seattle Presbytery less than a year earlier at the end of 2001 fresh out of grad school at the University of Minnesota. My wife, Adrienne, had accepted a call to serve as a chaplain at the Seattle Cancer Care Alliance. And she grew up in the Seattle area. So, it made sense to head west. But there was a lot about my life at the time that didn't make as much sense.

It was not long after 9/11 that challenged my assumptions of security and my assumptions about how people from other countries and backgrounds perceived the United States. Call me naïve, but the idea that a whole network of people could orchestrate subduing the crews of several commercial airline flights at the same time and successfully fly these massive planes into the Twin Towers, the Pentagon, and other highly symbolic targets was both terrifying and remarkable.

The afternoon of the 9/11 attacks was when I interviewed with Rev. Boyd Stockdale and Daisy Dawson at the Seattle Presbytery. They said yes! The following Sunday, September 16, after months of battling recurrent ear infections in our amazing one-and-a-half-year-old daughter Maya, we went to the hospital and refused to leave until they could tell us what was going on with her. We knew it wasn't just ear infections. That day shifted our sense of what it meant to be parents as our beautiful girl began three years of waves of treatments for leukemia. We are so grateful that this year we get to celebrate her marriage to a fine young man and she is thriving in life. But at that time, over dim sum with Fred in sunny south Seattle, we had no idea what would happen.

And I was being honest that I had never heard of Darrell Guder. You see, in the Department of Communication Studies of the University of Minnesota where I was blessed to study with one of my heroes, Dr. Robert L. Scott, we didn't much care about theologians. Spivak, Foucault, Derrida, and Habermas were the thought leaders in that domain. Who's Guder? And resorting to "God" as a legitimate explanation for the creativity, movement, connection, insight, and comprehension that can happen in the act of communicating was just lazy!

Fred, who was serving at Summit Avenue Presbyterian Church across Puget Sound in the city of Bremerton, most well known for Navy base Kitsap Bremerton, shared more about his plan for inviting Darrell to speak and why. So, I went with it.

While we were prepping for him to come Fred made sure I got my hands on his latest book, *The Continuing Conversion of the Church* (2000).[1] I distinctly remember learning the title and my spirit doing a less visible version of the dog cocking its head to the side in a gesture

---

1. Guder, *Continuing Conversion of the Church*.

of "huh?" Conversion of the church? Aren't we the community of the convert-ed? Why would the church need converting? And why continuously? You have to remember I hadn't heard of Darrell at that point, hadn't read *Missional Church*.[2] Heck, I hadn't heard the word "missional."

Then he came and spoke. It was early 2003 on a Saturday morning in an educational lounge at Seattle First Presbyterian Church in the heart of downtown Seattle. And it clicked.

Darrell's talk was the first time I heard the perspective that we, disciples of Jesus in the church, are in need of continuing conversion. And that clicked in place for me! His simple yet ground-shakingly profound insight was that the gospel of Jesus Christ was actually a message, a critique, good news to turn back on ourselves. We who called ourselves Christian were the target audience for the gospel of Jesus who calls us to become apostolic!

Darrell the Apostolicity Reclaimer

That talk in 2003 was the first time that I heard about the qualities of apostolicity . . . say that five times fast. Not just apost*les* . . . as in the guys in *Acts* . . . but apostolicity . . . as in you and me and others who embody apostolic gifts. That a congregation, a church is not an entity who possesses a mission that it enacts onto others. It is God who is on a mission and has a church to embody God's mission. The more we get the source of agency wrong, the more we miss what God is trying to accomplish.

I also remember him reflecting on something I had not, at the time, fully understood. Darrell was on faculty and even short-term president at Whitworth University, a Presbyterian-affiliated school in Spokane, Washington, that began in the greater Seattle-Tacoma area in the 1800s and then moved across the mountains. So, he was steeped in Presbyterian history in the West. And he shared with us that morning that we were sitting in the lounge of the church that eighty years earlier was the largest Presbyterian church in the country. It may have been the largest Protestant church at that time, claiming over ten thousand members in the 1930s.

By 2002 when he was speaking there it claimed about four hundred members. That congregation has since dissolved. But that day when Darrell came to speak, I saw myself as a disciple of Jesus from a whole new

---

2. Guder, *Missional Church*.

point of view. I was invited to recognize that apostles weren't contained just in the book of Acts, that I was one, that we were alive today. That God's mission has a church and when we are in sync with God's mission in the world, we can be useful. When we think our role is to play church who has a mission, all sorts of things lose life! My vocabulary got a boost that day. My faith got caffeinated.

Darrell the Encourager

I didn't think Darrell would remember me from that day, but eight years later, after I had been called to serve as executive presbyter of the Northwest Coast Presbytery, a judicatory of PC-USA just north of Seattle, he came to speak to a national gathering of presbytery staff persons. He had much the same message, but this time he helped us see presbytery leadership as an apostolic activity. It was the first time I heard the idea that the apostle Paul might have been the first executive presbyter (EP)—a person called to exercise spiritual leadership with a "presbytery"-like entity. A presbytery is a group of ministers of word and sacrament, congregations, fellowships, new worshiping communities in a geographic region of the Presbyterian Church USA.

I went up to him afterward to say hello and thank him for his teaching. He said, "You're welcome. And weren't you my host some years ago in Seattle for a talk I gave there?"

"Yep, that's me. I'm surprised you remember," I replied. "I've taken on a new role with a neighboring presbytery as EP." "I've been hearing good things about what you and the presbytery are doing out there," Darrell shared. I probably had that same head-cocked dog look. "Huh? . . . uh . . . yeah, I guess we are," I replied. That's when I got the inkling there's more going on here than a brilliant scholar sharing his knowledge. There's someone who notices, and remembers, and appreciates . . . personally.

Jump ahead a few years to 2013. The presbytery I served was in the process of merging together with the presbytery in southeast Alaska. As I was flying from Seattle to Juneau one time and looking down on the coastlands of British Columbia, I got curious about what the Presbyterians in British Columbia, Canada, were up to. When I got home from that trip I grew determined to make some connections with our siblings in Christ in British Columbia. After a few serendipitous connections I joined another pastor from our presbytery for a drive up to Vancouver, where I was blessed to meet Rev. Dr. Ross Lockhart of St. Andrews Hall. Ross is a prolific theologian and writer, a winsome and engaging teacher and storyteller, and a spirit-driven preacher, and he has quite a knack for creating connections and making new ministry life happen. At the time, he was starting up the Centre for Missional Leadership at St. Andrews Hall and has since assumed the deanship.

He was in the process of connecting with Darrell Guder as a theologian in residence for the Centre, and in that process both Ross and I got invited to Princeton Theological Seminary during Darrell's last year before retiring. We were part of a group invited to come and give insight and shape to a new initiative Princeton was considering. When we arrived with others from our delegation, Darrell and his wife Judy invited us to their home for a welcome dinner. They were so warm and hospitable, eager to hear what we were learning, and grateful to share their lives with us and show us the seminary and introduce us to their friends and colleagues. We had a great time that evening and during the consultation.

What I observed about Darrell in that setting was the kind of respectful, caring, and challenge-rich relationship he had with several of his students and former students who were also there for the consultation. In addition to being their professor and advisor, he had a strong personal connection with them, a mentoring relationship in which, now that they were practicing ministry, he saw them as equals, colleagues in this ministry. And I saw how he treated his professor colleagues as insightful contributors to this amazing enterprise called the gospel of Jesus Christ.

I could see that in his last years before retiring he was actively cultivating a next generation of scholars and pastoral leaders. "Darrell is coming to teach our elders and deacons!" Following retirement Darrell and Judy relocated to the Seattle area, where I live, and we've had more opportunity to connect both at St. Andrews Hall and through the presbytery that I served previously.

I wanted that same kind of shift of perspective on what it means to be a church who is part of God's mission rather than a church with a mission that he got me going on back in 2002, for the congregations I served. When partnering with one of our churches in Bellingham, Washington, for officer training, I had the thought that I should just reach out to Darrell and see if he'd be open to offering teaching to one congregation's elders and deacons. I suspected it was a long shot, but I had to try. And sure enough, he jumped at the opportunity. And he did so out of a conviction; I remember him saying something like "these elders and deacons are the front line of Christian ministry, and if I can make a contribution to their ministry, I need to do that."

The pastor of that congregation, Rev. Greg Ellis, said one day something like, "I can't believe that Darrell Guder, *the* Darrell Guder, is gonna come to teach our elders and deacons. WOW!" My enduring gratitude for Darrell Guder is in part the legacy of scholarship and the way he and others helped flip the narrative and missional perspective of church right side up. But more than that, it is for his personal, caring, hospitable way of being in ministry with students, colleagues, and others while challenging each other to more insight and better ministry.

Still Flipping Minds in Retirement

One more flip . . . during one of Darrell's consultations with pastoral leaders at St. Andrews Hall in 2019 while he served as theologian-in-residence, he challenged us with an insight from the Nicene Creed. He took the Nicene Creed's line about the church, "One, Holy, Catholic and Apostolic church." And together with another scholar artfully flipped it to show what a more missional church might declare. We are apostolic first, catholic, holy, and therefore one. Instead of making unity the precursor to all the other markers, perhaps our apostolicity might be a better on-ramp to becoming one church.

He used this to illustrate a fundamental flip in perspective from a "Christendom" model church . . . we've gotta be one, believe similar, agree on matters of orthodoxy and from that springs holiness and apostolicity. To a missional flip where God is sending (*apostolos*) the church, you and me, into God's mission as we live that adventurous life, the Spirit has a way of weaving us into oneness! May it be so! Darrell, thank you for being an apostle in our lives blessing us and the whole church with your insight, scholarship, and your warm friendship, encouragement, and challenge! Who is Darrell? An apostle for this generation and generations to come! Thank you, Darrell Guder!

For Reflection

1. Reflect on Corey's evolving relationship with Darrell Guder. How important is mentorship in professional and personal development?

Can you identify a moment when a mentor's guidance significantly impacted your path?

2. Several of the authors in this book comment on Guder's concept of "continuing conversion of the church"; what does it mean to you? How does this idea challenge traditional views of the church and its mission?

3. Corey describes a shift in understanding the role of the church from possessing a mission to embodying God's mission. How does this perspective change the way you view the role of religious institutions and their leaders?

21

Through the Roof Medicine

Toby Long

It doesn't take a medical degree to see that healthcare today is not altogether healthy. Declining lifespans, increasing obesity, worsening rates of addiction, and chronic disease all suggest that the American healthcare system is sick. Where once it seemed that better medicine meant healthier patients, today it appears that new medicines can create healthier profit margins, but healthier patients are getting more difficult to find. As a physician, I have experienced times when the best we have to offer is not enough, and moments when the best that is available is not accessible to populations who need help most. If healthcare's mission is healing, then why all the spreading sickness in modern society and contemporary life?

For most of my professional career, I have worked as a family physician at a community health center in an underserved neighborhood. The vital signs I measure every day to assess the health of a patient's body do not measure vital aspects of a patient's well-being. I have yet to discover a vital sign for the soul. I've often wondered if something like this is possible. If not, the prognosis may be grim. My own life was not always preoccupied with science and sickness. Before attending medical school at Michigan State University, I had the pleasure of attending Princeton

Theological Seminary in the era of Professor Darrell Guder. When I entered seminary, I had the naive notion that mission was something I did for God. Praise be to God for Darrell Guder and the Missional Theology Seminar that set me straight.

I still remember my first class with Darrell Guder. Twice weekly in Stuart Hall, he gathered a mostly Reformed but decidedly ecumenical crowd for a two-hour, high-energy, prayer-laden, and German phrase–filled lecture that would be a missional reorientation of my theology and identity as a Christian called to mission. In that upper room, Dr. Guder reintroduced his students to the ancient idea of *missio Dei* and challenged us to see the church not as the object of our mission but as the instrument of God's mission. We learned to speak of God as a "missionary God" and the church as a "sent people." In every class, Dr. Guder reminded us of our missional mandate, "you shall be my witnesses," always with the refrain to "lead lives worthy of the calling to which you have been called." His recurring take home lesson: mission is God's work because mission is God's nature.

If *missio Dei* was a favored theme of Professor Guder's missional theology, a favorite verse was John 20:21, "As the Father has sent me, so I send you." In the booklet *Mission in Christ's Way* (1987), Lesslie Newbigin explains how Jesus sent his disciples out with the words of John 20:21. Newbigin concludes that in light of Christ's command, Christians are obliged to emulate Christ's ministry in our own ministry efforts; "we are not authorized to do it in any other way."[1] It is only natural to ask, what was the nature of Christ's mission and ministry? How did the Father send the Son? Newbigin suggests that in the mission of Jesus we see "both the presence of the kingdom and also the proclamation of the kingdom."[2] There is healing and there is proclamation. When the kingdom comes, the sick are made well and the blind are made to see. Preaching becomes an opportunity to explain healing as the coming of the kingdom of God. In this way, our words and our deeds are equally required, for only together can they embody the richness of God's love for us, body and soul, now and into eternity. Mission in Christ's way always resists the partisan tendency to reduce mission to either social justice and the needs of the body, or a "soul justice" preoccupied only with the question of an individual's eternal destiny. God's mission redeems all people, reconciles all

---

1. Newbigin, *Mission in Christ's Way*, 1.
2. Newbigin, *Mission in Christ's Way*, 10.

things, and heals all wounds. This attention to social justice *and* "soul justice" is doing mission in Christ's way.

Many years into my own medical practice, I often ask myself, is there a way to do missional medicine? Could a clinician follow Newbigin and Guder's lead, and do medicine in Christ's way? Even a cursory read of the Gospels will reveal that healing was a central part of Jesus' three-year ministry. Of the thirty-seven miracles Jesus performed in the Gospels, two-thirds involved healing. Healing was not merely important to Jesus; it took center stage whenever he chose to manifest the power of God. Without exception, every person in the Gospels who came to Jesus for healing was healed. In every instance, out of compassion, Jesus makes the decision to heal the sick or cast out the evil spirit. This is a scriptural fact worth noting. Healing is not a "side dish" in the Gospels or an appetizer to preaching of the kingdom of God. Healing is a main dish in Christ's ministry and a central feature of God's compassionate kingdom.

As a physician, I have a favorite healing passage. It's in two Gospels, Mark and Luke. In honor of St. Luke, the physician evangelist, I will include the healing of the paralytic from Luke 5:17–26:

> [17] One day, while he was teaching, Pharisees and teachers of the law were sitting nearby (they had come from every village of Galilee and Judea and from Jerusalem); and the power of the Lord was with him to heal. [18] Just then some men came, carrying a paralyzed man on a bed. They were trying to bring him in and lay him before Jesus; [19] but finding no way to bring him in because of the crowd, they went up on the roof and let him down with his bed through the tiles into the middle of the crowd in front of Jesus. [20] When he saw their faith, he said, "Friend, your sins are forgiven you." [21] Then the scribes and the Pharisees began to question, "Who is this who is speaking blasphemies? Who can forgive sins but God alone?" [22] When Jesus perceived their questionings, he answered them, "Why do you raise such questions in your hearts? [23] Which is easier, to say, 'Your sins are forgiven you,' or to say, 'Stand up and walk'? [24] But so that you may know that the Son of Man has authority on earth to forgive sins"—he said to the one who was paralyzed—"I say to you, stand up and take your bed and go to your home." [25] Immediately he stood up before them, took what he had been lying on, and went to his home, glorifying God.

It is worth noting that we are only in the fifth chapter of Luke's Gospel, and already, this is the fourth account of Jesus healing somebody. It doesn't take long for mission to happen. In this passage we meet a group of friends who are carrying a paralytic on a bed. It must have been quite a sight. The passage describes how crowds pressed in and around the miracle man, Jesus of Nazareth. Everyone is jostling for a better position, standing tip-toed for a chance to glimpse a moment of the glory. At the back, a group of above average do-gooders are looking for an opportunity to get their sick friend closer to the action.

In this story, the goal was to get the sick man to Jesus. In life, the path to healing is often difficult and requires great effort and energy. For the paralytic, the path to Jesus was much the same. There were many obstacles. First, the friends had to figure out how to get a paralyzed man, lying on his bed, onto a roof. Then, they had to get this same man through the roof, to the floor near Jesus. This may well be the first miracle of this miraculous story. Amid all the buzz and busyness, the friends managed all of this and cautiously lowered the paralytic down to Jesus. I have tried to imagine their ingenuity, tenacity, and know-how many times. It is unlikely they anticipated the obstacles they would face; yet they found a way to get their friend through the roof to the One who was his best chance to walk again.

By the time the paralytic reached the ground, all eyes must have been on the encounter. The paralytic was likely anxious, certainly unable to move. Peering down through the roof, the tired and dusty faced friends were watching with wide-eyed excitement and anticipation hoping they'd have the best seat in the house for the best miracle in Capernaum. Standing in the middle of it all was Jesus. He saw the great effort made on behalf of this paralyzed man, which Jesus is quick to describe as faith (v. 19). In response to their faith, Jesus looks at the paralyzed man and says something nobody expects, "Friend, your sins are forgiven." Sins? Jesus' first move in this moment of great effort and faith was to heal the paralytic's sins. Imagine the shock, dismay, and even disappointment all around. I doubt the friends on the roof were thinking about sin when they lowered the paralytic to Jesus. I can see them watching from above, heads shaking, and brows furrowed, wanting to shout aloud, "No! Rabbi, please! We're glad for the sin forgiveness and all, but did you see his legs? His body is broken! He needs healing!"

The scribes and Pharisees also appear to have been caught off guard. The Scripture makes their dismay clear as they rebuke Jesus asking, "Who is this speaking blasphemies? Who can heal sins but God alone?" Jesus accepts their question but not their condemnation. He is not looking for a theological debate; he is God's kingdom looking to heal a sick sinner. Jesus replies, "Which is easier to say, 'Your sins are forgiven' or 'stand up and walk?' But so that you may know that the Son of Man has authority on earth to forgive sins, I say to you, stand up and take your bed and go to your home." When everyone wanted to see a body healed, Jesus made a soul new *and* then he made a body whole again. There is no halfway fix in the kingdom of God. When "the power of the Lord was with him to heal," Jesus made *all things* new.

This healing of the whole—body and soul—is a trademark of mission in Christ's way. While everyone in the passage is focused on the paralytic's body, Christ tends to his soul. Jesus deals first with the man's unseen sickness. Then, he reveals the heart of the Father who wants to fix it all by telling this forgiven sinner to stand up, take his mat, and walk home. Churches may work to save souls and hospitals can work to heal bodies, but when Jesus heals, he heals it all.

What if the story of the healing of the paralytic could serve as a model for missional medicine and a paradigm for how to do medicine in Christ's way? What if medicine could follow Christ's example and address not only the needs of the body, but of the soul as well? A missional model of healthcare would require a shift in our understanding of who we are in life and what we are in fact as human creatures. As we see in Scripture, when Jesus heals a man, he heals the whole—body and soul. Following Christ in this way, missional medicine would be a truly holistic endeavor by seeing the material needs of the body with the spiritual reality of the soul. Following the example of Luke 5, we might call this missional model of healthcare "Through the Roof Medicine." Like Jesus in the healing of the paralytic, Through the Roof Medicine incorporates the invisible reality of a soul in every visible body that presents for care.

In the opening line of his book *Peace of Soul*, Bishop Fulton Sheen writes, "Unless souls are saved, nothing is saved."[3] Christian tradition teaches that souls are inseparably united to bodies and that it is only in death that the soul separates from the body. In life, the soul and the body are one. Human beings are a unified duality of body and soul, one person made in the image and likeness of God. Therefore, it reasons that to save the soul, one might want to care for the body, and in caring for the body, it would be negligent to forget the soul that animates the body and makes it alive.

---

3. Sheen, *Peace of Soul*, 1.

Both Aristotle and Aquinas believed in the existence of a soul. According to Aristotle, the soul is the form of the body. It is the substance that makes a thing to be what it is and the animating force that gives a thing life. In *De Anima* 2.1 he writes, "What it is to be an axe would be its substance, and this would also be its soul."[4] Aristotle argues that the soul is not the matter of a thing itself, but the form.[5] He illustrates this stating, "If an eye were an animal, its soul would be sight."[6] The soul is what makes a thing to be what it is. The soul animates a thing to perform the activity for which it exists. In this way, one cannot divide soul and body without changing the essence of a body. Pointing to the essential unity of body and soul, Aristotle states that "it is unnecessary to inquire whether the soul and body are one, just as it is unnecessary to ask this concerning the wax and its seal."[7]

This is Aristotle's principle of hylomorphism, the idea that every physical object is a unified composite of matter and form.[8] Applying this principle to people, the soul is the immaterial coordinating reality that organizes the matter into a human being and animates the person into the state of being alive. Following Aristotle's lead, Thomas Aquinas believed the soul to be primary, that which gives the whole of the body its unity and form.[9] The soul exists by virtue of itself and the body by virtue of the soul. Following Aquinas, Christian tradition has taught that the unity of the soul and body is so profound that one concludes the soul to be the form of the body and the body to be the matter of the soul. We are a single substance that is both material and spiritual.[10] The soul is the form that actualizes the body into living matter.

In Latin, soul is *anima* from which we derive "animate," and so we understand that the soul animates the body, akin to a deeply integrated life-forming force that makes a body to be alive. If our soul is separated from our body, we experience death. If there is no soul, there is no life, even if all the parts of the body remain. A corpse is not a person.

---

4. Aristotle, *De Anima* 412b13–14.
5. Aristotle, *De Anima* 412a15–22.
6. Aristotle, *De Anima* 412b18.
7. Aristotle, *De Anima* 412b7–9.
8. Editors of Encyclopedia Britannica, "Hylomorphism."
9. Aquinas, *Summa Theologica* art. 8, q. 76, "Union of Soul and Body in Man."
10. Kreeft, *Practical Theology*, 324.

If the soul makes the body into a living thing, one might conclude that anything that strengthens the soul may benefit the body. In the same way, one might see how neglect of the body is detrimental to the soul. Perhaps this is why St. Paul writes that sins against the body are so serious.[11] It is not hard to look at the state of the world today and wonder if the practical atheism and materialism flourishing in our postmodern, post-Christian culture might play a part in the remarkable rise in chronic disease,[12] depression,[13] suicide,[14] and addiction.[15] Are we losing our health and our mind because we have lost touch with the reality of our soul?

Admittedly, it seems overzealous to imagine a medical model that acknowledges the reality of a soul. There are not many in science or medicine who will take seriously ideas that are immaterial and unmeasurable. Perhaps it is worth remembering times past when we did not know what we know today and did not treat what we could not see. It was not until the nineteenth century that a scientist first described a germ theory to explain the "invisible," but real, cause of various human infection and disease. The French chemist Louis Pasteur proposed his theory to the French Medical Academy in 1878 to finally explain how microscopic germs like bacteria and viruses were the cause of so much sickness.[16] Germ theory is now regarded as one of the most important discoveries in the history of medicine. Germ theory challenged the medical profession to reevaluate what it believed about the cause and origin of human illness and inspired a revolution in medical technology, treatment, and disease prevention.

Today, we are indebted to the work of scientists like Louis Pasteur (d. 1895) and Robert Koch (d. 1910) who opened our eyes to a world we cannot see. We no longer rebalance bodily humors; we wash our hands and sanitize our surgical instruments. We no longer bleed an infection; we prescribe an antibiotic. Germ theory was a monumental revolution in medical understanding and practice. Could "soul theory" do something similar for medicine today? Once again, could that which is unseen, but

---

11. 1 Cor 6:18–20.

12. Hacker, "Burden of Chronic Disease," 112–19.

13. Santomauro et al., "Global Prevalence and Burden," 1700–12; Dykxhoorn et al., "Temporal Patterns in the Recorded Annual Incidence," 1–12.

14. Simon and Masters, "Institutional Failures as Structural Determinants of Suicide."

15. Substance Abuse and Mental Health Services Administration, *Key Substance Use*.

16. Horgan, "Germ Theory."

real, become a recognized part of what needs attention, treatment, and care? Could a reintegration of an ancient anthropology open the door to therapeutic alternatives that provide care for the soul in a manner similar to how medicine treats the body today?

As a cardinal in the Roman Catholic Church, Joseph Ratzinger wrote extensively on the philosophical theology of the human person.[17] At his inauguration mass at St. Peter's Square, newly ordained Pope Benedict XVI declared, "We are not some casual and meaningless product of evolution. Each of us is the result of a thought of God. Each of us is willed, each of us is loved, each of us is necessary."[18] Created by God, we bear God's image in ourselves as something that is both body and soul. Following the foundation set by Aristotle and Aquinas, the Catholic Church concludes, "The unity of soul and body is so profound that one has to consider the soul to be the 'form' of the body: i.e., it is because of its spiritual soul that the body made of matter becomes a living, human body; spirit and matter, in man, are not two natures united, but rather their union forms a single nature."[19]

Such logic would lead to a medical model that considers how to heal the soul even as it treats the body. If the soul is there, and we fail to see it, we are like a doctor trying to treat chest pain while having no concept of the heart.

Most people will need something more concrete than what can be had from Aquinas or some papal ponderings on the nature of the soul. "Show me the evidence" is a popular refrain in medicine today. Admittedly, studying the impact of religion and prayer on health and healing is tricky. There have been attempts to look for a connection between faith and health or prayer and healing.[20] Recently, a professor of epidemiology at Harvard T. H. Chan School of Public Health, Tyler VanderWeele, wrote in *Harvard Public Health*:

> Extrapolations from the Nurses' Health Study data suggest that about 40 percent of the increasing suicide rate in the United States from 1999 to 2014 might be attributed to declines in attendance at religious services during this period.[21]

17. Ratzinger, "Concerning the Notion of Person."
18. Benedict XVI, "Homily," para. 6.
19. *Catechism of the Catholic Church*, §365.
20. Center for Spirituality, Theology, and Health at Duke University, https://spiritualityandhealth.duke.edu/.
21. VanderWeele, Li, and Kawachi, "Religious Service Attendance and Suicide Rates," 197–98.

Another study suggested declining attendance from 1991 to 2019 accounted for 28 percent of the increase in depression among adolescents.[22] VanderWeele goes on to note,

> A major 2022 systematic review in the *Journal of the American Medical Association* documented 215 studies, each with sample sizes over 1,000 participants, using longitudinal data to evaluate the relationship between religion and health.[23] The evidence from meta-analyses, large longitudinal studies (including from Harvard's own Nurses' Health Study) and handbooks providing more extensive documentation, suggests that weekly religious service attendance is longitudinally associated with lower mortality risk, lower depression, less suicide, better cardiovascular disease survival, better health behaviors, and greater marital stability, happiness, and purpose in life.[24]

Studies like these suggest that prayer has the power to improve health, and religious service attendance may benefit mental wellbeing and quality of life on statistically significant levels. Of course, there is nothing in these data that can prove the existence of a soul. However, the data do imply that activities one might call "soul care" may benefit the body and give traditional "healthcare" a bit of healthy competition.

With our missional heroes, the brave friends of the paralytic, the goal of "Through the Roof Medicine" is to get the sick to Jesus. This model welcomes all that modern science and technology have to offer while simultaneously listening to the philosophical wisdom of the ancients and the theological truths of Christian Scripture and tradition. "Through the Roof Medicine" desires to mend everything that is broken and treat all that needs healing. It rejects a reductionistic "either/or" approach to healthcare and embraces a "both/and" approach to healing that treats the body and the soul with every available resource. Whether it be pharmaceutical, psychological, surgical, or spiritual, this approach is as happy to write a prescription as it is to bow the head in a prayer for a patient's healing.

Having become Catholic since my time at Princeton Theological Seminary, I have learned what most already know: not all Catholics are

---

22. Kreski et al., "Explaining US Adolescent Depressive Symptom Trends," 300–326.

23. Balboni et al., "Spirituality in Serious Illness and Health," 184–97.

24. Chen, Kim, and VanderWeele, "Religious-Service Attendance and Subsequent Health," 2030–40.

saints. Having come out of the rich heritage of the Reformed faith, I also know that not all saints are Catholic. I have deep confidence that Professor Guder is one of those special scholar saints whose own faith has informed his study and whose faithful teaching has formed his students for mission. I am inexpressibly grateful to Dr. Guder for his energetic witness and faithful scholarship. While saints from both sides of the Tiber have yet to live into the unity for which Christ prayed (John 17:20–23), Christians of every kind can unite around the call to be a saint. For a saint is someone whose life is about one thing.[25] That one thing is the universal call to missionary discipleship where the faithful have done (and are doing) mission in Christ's way. If such saints find themselves in healthcare, perhaps they might consider doing medicine "through the roof," by getting the sick to Jesus, who can heal it all, the body in this life and the soul in preparation for the life to come.

For Reflection

1. Dr. Long writes about the relationship between soul and body. Did you grow up believing the soul to be more important?

2. What is your vocation? What does it mean to do missional _____ (fill in your vocation or occupation)?

3. What or who needs healing? In your own life? In your faith community? In your neighborhood? How do we bring those prayers "through the roof"?

---

25. Kierkegaard. *Purity of Heart*, 5.

Afterword

Mark Glanville

While this is not the first book I have read that honors a learned scholar, it is certainly the first packed full of stories about meals, mentoring, hospitality, and transformative teaching. It is also the first packed full of the personal impact Darrell Guder has had on pastors and their churches, churches which bear witness to Christ in their neighborhoods.

For example, Thomas Daniel tells us in his chapter how, as a new student at Columbia, he nervously approached Darrell's office: "[Darrell] introduced himself, invited me to sit down, and wanted to learn more about my journey to seminary. For about forty-five minutes he gave me his full and undivided attention and I spoke without pausing for breath." He adds, "We began having a standing weekly breakfast together for almost three years, until Darrell left for Princeton Theological Seminary." How inspiring this is for all who pastor, mentor, and teach! Is it not tempting to bump that coffee or breakfast with a mentee in order to carve out a little more writing time? Thomas Daniel sees in Darrell an "alignment between what he teaches and how he lives."

In a similar way, Kurt Helmcke speaks of Darrell's relational, incarnational way of shepherding. Darrell's example formed Kurt to see pastoral ministry as a highly relational activity of "guiding people . . . into the sending flow of God's love." While I myself have not had the closeness of friendship with Darrell expressed by many throughout this book, I have been blessed by his company in the ongoing journey of the Gospel and

Our Culture Network. Darrell, along with others in his cohort, birthed this scholarly network to support the witness of the church through research, writing, and speaking. This group shares a conviction that witness isn't merely one task that the church must do; rather witness is the very identity of the church. Jesus made this clear after his resurrection, when he said to his disciples: "As the Father sent me, I am sending you" (John 20:21). Therefore, everything we do as a church is to display Jesus' tender lordship within our neighborhood—from prayer, to worship, to justice-seeking, to maintaining our building, to speaking about Jesus.

Such a broad and beautiful vision for witness sharply challenges the individualistic, other-worldly focus that so often characterizes church life. In his chapter, Ross Lockhart captures Darrell's critique of the ways that the church all too often prunes away beauty from the church's witness: "The church trims the gospel to fit the culture, reducing Christian action to little more than a 'salvation management system,' regulating sin while being consumed with an emphasis on the afterlife." In contrast, Scripture shapes the church to bear witness to God's healing work for all of the creation and for every aspect of human life within it. We do this by "being the witness, saying the witness, and doing the witness"—I regularly quote this three-part phrase by Darrell in my classes. We can (and should) read the Bible missionally, as the story of God's setting out to redeem the creation, calling a people to live as a sign to God's restorative reign in Christ.

Some readers of this book who are reflecting on reading the Bible missionally for the first time may feel overwhelmed by the complexity of this approach, especially since in this book Darrell's missional theology is expressed by many voices, in a narrative style. Given this possibility, I especially appreciate Andrea Perrett's reflection that Darrell's influence "has embedded a 'missional' approach so deeply that it has gotten into my bones." There is a lot of wisdom here. We need to soak in this missional reading of Scripture over years—and especially to live it out—until it has gotten into our bones. Just think: every book of the Bible was written to form a community of God's people to be salt and light in their original, ancient context! We can soak that in, until we read the Bible that way every time we pick it up. After a while, we will become amazed once again at Scripture's radical invitation for our church community: *we are invited to play a part in God's story of redemption, embodying the tenderness of Jesus in our neighborhood!*

For me, the highlight of this book is the ways in which Darrell's missional theology and shepherding presence have inspired fresh, on-the-ground, expressions of the kingdom of God. Consider Renée and James B Notkin's story of launching Union Church Seattle in 2006. They observed that "the growing emphasis in the North American church on transactional sin management rather than transformative living contributed to a community of exhausted and discouraged believers." They decided to chart a different path. Instead of finding a traditional church building, they created a "third space" where their broader local community could gather. They called their space 415 Westlake instead of Union Church, "because of our desire to communicate steadfastly that we, God's people, are the church. The building is where we gather to be sent." Renée and James shared how the term "witness" triggered their people, summoning memories of street evangelists and other outdated cultural oddities. They write that when Darrell visited their community, "There was excitement, scratching of heads, wonder, doubt, and perplexity as Darrell emphatically, yet kindly, encouraged us to not forsake the word 'witness' but rather to reclaim Christ's definition, as the One who invites: 'You shall be my witnesses.'"

Similarly, Albert Chu shares that when he and his team started Tapestry Church, Vancouver, they had a key leader allocated for each church ministry. There was a key leader for children's ministry, another for finance, and so on. However, Tap Church deliberately didn't appoint a key leader for witness, reasoning that every ministry of the church was to be oriented around witness. Inspired by Darrell's book *Missional Church*, Tap Church is shaping their shared life to reflect the reality that witness is the very identity of the church, and so it infuses everything we do. Every ministry nourishes God's people to display Jesus' tender reign.

Then there is Tim Dickau's description of the incarnational practices in Grandview Church, Vancouver, which were partly inspired by Darrell's writings. Grandview Church reordered the patterns shaping the church's life. Many parishioners at Grandview moved into houses and apartments a short walk from the church, creating a warm parish feel. "These structures facilitated the development of common practices in the *natural rhythm of our lives* and allowed us to form a more porous community that included our neighbors," Tim writes. Tim describes the call on the church at this time as a "shift from a Christendom model of offering spiritual services towards the forming of an incarnational community that participates in the fuller mission of God's kingdom come in a particular place." Grandview developed a variety of social enterprises and NGOs in East Vancouver, including Kinbrace, a leading NGO welcoming refugee-ed people.

Being an incarnational community in a neighborhood requires slowing down and listening to our community. Slowing and listening is key for Preston Pouteaux's ministry in Chestermere, Alberta. Preston tells us how beekeeping helped him to grasp the value of being a gentle presence in his neighborhood. "Gentle proximity to the bees is what makes a beekeeper. You must draw near, and the bees will teach you and reshape your imagination. They will give you signs of health and sickness, and in time you will know how to care for them, but you have to lean in. Listen. Touch. Wait. Act. Maybe even love them." Preston discovered that taking on the same posture in his pastoral work in Chestermere created space for trust and intimacy to develop with his neighbors.

Yet another example of incarnational witness is The Children's Garden Collective, started by Konnie Vissers in Hamilton, Ontario. The Children's Garden Collective fosters children's development by addressing food insecurity though urban gardening. Konnie's work is truly "witness in life, word, and deed," as Darrell puts it. Konnie reflects: "We did not seek to convert our neighbors, but as Darrell so often referenced the words of John Mackay, we had 'earned the right to be heard.'"

As we read through these lived-out stories of incarnation, we can't help but be struck that the triune God is the centering reality which unites each of them. Fresh expressions of church, which engage culture with tenderness, are grounded by our union with the Son, who sends us. They are birthed from a desire to partner with the Creator, at the Creator's invitation, in healing the world. And they are animated by the creativity of the Spirit. Many of the contributors to this book express how the triune God is the heart and source of Darrell's life and teaching.

A final lesson I will mention from these essays is the value of remaining open to learning and growing throughout our lives. I recall strolling through the maple tree–lined streets of the University of British Columbia with Darrell ten years ago. I asked his opinion about a controversial issue facing the Vancouver church at the time. Darrell simply responded that he wasn't sure about what to think. He said, "I think it's going to take us the next fifty years to learn about that issue." Darrell's response strikes me as remarkably wise. While my question created space for a brilliant answer—surely the way of learned scholars—Darrell instead chose to suspend judgment and to resist the opportunity to pour forth knowledge.

In the same vein, Sarah Bixler shares the story of Darrell's pencil to illustrate his capacity to change. Darrell would input appointments into his diary in pencil only: "That way I can change them as needed," he reasoned. Sarah reflects on Darrell's attachment to pencils: "I came to recognize that this was not just an approach to calendar keeping. Darrell ordered his life, work, teaching, scholarship, and theology around the assumption that they were all open to change."

Reading through these chapters, we witness Darrell's capacity to change throughout the various periods of his vocational and intellectual life. I was struck, for example, by Sarah's description of a lecture in which Darrell observed the "sad reality that power usually defines unity." Once you have read those words, it's obvious: of course, power defines unity! But to say it in the first place, to think into the idea that *power usually defines unity*, and to build a lecture on it, surely requires a readiness to learn and to grow. To have this insight, Darrell would have had to stay soft, to embody the humility to critique ecclesial power, a power that he himself shares.

As I pen the final words of this rich volume, I am aware of my longing—I might say my ache—to be nurtured by leaders who have traveled further down the road of life. I am now fifty years old. Where are the older, wiser folk with the capacity to love us and cheer us on without fear, as we chart a rough course through this new cultural moment? This volume demonstrates how Darrell has been one of those people for many of us. Darrell has played that role not only because of his great learning and vast ministry experience, but through his readiness to listen and to learn—through his curiosity and love.

Contributors

SARAH BIXLER is associate professor of formation and practical theology and associate dean of the Seminary at Eastern Mennonite University. She holds a PhD in practical theology from Princeton Theological Seminary.

JASON BYASSEE is senior minister at Timothy Eaton Memorial Church in Toronto and a senior fellow of CML.

ALBERT Y. S. CHU served as the director of the Centre for Missional Leadership until December 2024 and is the founding pastor of the Tapestry Church in Vancouver, BC.

CHRIS CURRIE is senior pastor at St. Charles Avenue Presbyterian Church in New Orleans, Louisiana. He holds a PhD in theology from the University of Edinburgh and has served churches in North Carolina and Louisiana. He is the author of *The Only Sacrament Left to Us* (Wipf & Stock), articles in *Journal for Preachers* and the Pro Ecclesia Series (Wipf & Stock), and he teaches Reformed theology and Presbyterian worship and polity at Duke Divinity School.

THOMAS DANIEL serves as the senior pastor of Covenant Presbyterian Church in Austin, Texas. He has also served as co-pastor and head of staff at First Presbyterian Church in Evanston, Illinois, as well as organizing co-pastor of an Atlanta church plant called Kairos Church, which quickly grew from seven to more than three hundred people.

TIM DICKAU is an associate at the Centre for Missional Leadership and the director of Citygate, an organization that fosters collaboration among churches to address systemic issues such as unaffordable housing, poverty, and refugees. He is also the author of *Forming Christian Communities in a Secular Age* and *Plunging into the Kingdom Way*.

MARK GLANVILLE holds a PhD from Trinity College, Bristol, and is ordained in The Presbyterian Church of Australia. Mark recently served as the associate professor of pastoral theology at Regent College and is author of several books including *Preaching in a New Key: Crafting Expository Sermons in Post-Christian Communities* and *Improvising Church: Scripture as the Source of Harmony, Rhythm, and Soul*. Mark was appointed the new director of the Centre for Missional Leadership at St. Andrew's Hall on January 1, 2025.

KURT HELMCKE is a pastor in Mill Creek, Washington. He was a student of Darrell's at Whitworth University and Louisville Theological Seminary. Kurt can often be found paddle-boarding local waters with his wife Chrystal.

DAVID JENNINGS practiced law in Vancouver for over three decades. He held numerous leadership roles within the Presbyterian Church in Canada and several Christian charities. He now resides with his wife in Bermuda.

KEAS KEASLER is associate professor of spiritual theology and the director of the MA in Christian Spiritual Formation and Leadership at Friends University. He holds a PhD from Vrije Universiteit Amsterdam, serves as a research affiliate of the Dallas Willard Research Center at Westmont College, and is the author of the forthcoming book *Kingdom Apprenticeship: Dallas Willard's Formational Theology and Missional Vision* (IVP Academic). He and his wife, Sarah, and their three children live in Wichita, Kansas.

DOUG KELLY is the pastor of Bethany Presbyterian Church in Seattle, Washington. He is married to Jean Fandl-Kelly and they have three adult children.

Contributors

Ross A. Lockhart is the dean of St. Andrew's Hall and professor of mission studies at Vancouver School of Theology. Ross holds a PhD from Vrije Universiteit, Amsterdam, and is the author of several books including his most recent publication *West Coast Mission: The Changing Nature of Christianity in Vancouver* published by McGill-Queen's University Press. Ross lives with his family on Bowen Island, BC.

Toby Long is a happily married father of six who loves Jesus, soccer, and practicing the abstract art of medicine as the medical director of primary care for Great Lakes Bay Health Centers and as a core faculty member at Central Michigan University's family medicine residency in Saginaw, Michigan.

David J. "Monty" Montgomery is an Irish Presbyterian minister who is currently the European regional director for IFES. He is an alumnus of Regent College, Vancouver, and Covenant Theological Seminary, where he received his DMin on bivocational church planting.

Renee and James B Notkin serve together as co-pastors at Union Church, a PCUSA congregation they planted in the South Lake Union neighborhood of Seattle, Washington.

Andrea Perrett is an associate for New Witnessing Communities with the Centre for Missional Leadership in Vancouver, BC. As a multi-vocational church planter, Andrea can also be found proclaiming the gospel on a side of a mountain, during an online bread-baking circle, or from a pulpit when filling in at local congregations.

Preston Pouteaux is the pastor of Lake Ridge Community Church in Chestermere, Alberta. He is the author of several books including *The Bees of Rainbow Falls: Finding Faith, Imagination and Delight in Your Neighbourhood*.

Corey C. Schlosser-Hall, PhD, serves as deputy executive director of the Interim Unified Agency of the Presbyterian Church (U.S.A.), following fifteen years as executive presbyter for the Northwest Coast Presbytery. His executive leadership draws on diverse experiences as university faculty, wilderness guide, entrepreneur, and consultant.

Christoph Schneider, born in 1982, is married, has three kids, and lives in Calw, a town in the state of Baden-Württemberg. He loves being close to God and close to people. He currently serves as a youth pastor with "Young Life Partnership" in the EJW (Evangelisches Jugendwerk in Württemberg), the youth ministry of the Lutheran Church of Württemberg.

Grant Vissers is husband to Konnie and dad to three wonderful girls, and he currently serves as lead pastor at Kortright Presbyterian Church in Guelph, Canada. He likes brewing coffee slowly and trail running even slower.

Konnie Vissers is a beloved child of God, trying to impart hope to the next generation through her work as a mom, wife, pastor, gardener, researcher, and writer. She serves as sessional faculty at Knox College, University of Toronto, and Lutheran Theological Seminary of Saskatoon, where she teaches field education, human development, and historical theology.

Jonathan R. Wilson is senior consultant for Theological Integration, Canadian Baptist Ministries and senior research fellow, Centre for Missional Leadership, St. Andrew's Hall, UBC.

Bibliography

Abraham, William J. *The Logic of Evangelism*. Grand Rapids: Eerdmans, 1989.
Aquinas, Thomas. *Summa Theologica*. Translated by Fathers of the English Dominican Province. Benzinger, 1947. https://www.ccel.org/a/aquinas/summa/home.html.
Aristotle. *De Anima*. Translated by Christopher Shields. Clarendon Aristotle Series. Oxford: Oxford University Press, 2016.
Bakker, Karen. *Gaia's Web*. Cambridge: MIT Press, 2024.
Balboni, T. A., et al. "Spirituality in Serious Illness and Health." *Journal of the American Medical Association* 328.2 (2022) 184–97. doi:10.1001/jama.2022.11086.
"Baptism, Eucharist, and Ministry." Faith and Order Paper No. 111 [The "Lima Text"]. Geneva: World Council of Churches, 1982. https://www.oikoumene.org/resources/documents/baptism-eucharist-and-ministry-faith-and-order-paper-no-111-the-lima-text.
Barth, Karl. *Church Dogmatics*. 1/1: *The Doctrine of the Word of God*. Edited by G. W. Bromiley and T. F. Torrance. Translated by G. W. Bromiley. 2nd ed. Edinburgh: T&T Clark, 1975.
———. *Church Dogmatics*. 4/3.2: *The Doctrine of Reconciliation*. Edited by G. W. Bromley and T. F. Torrance. Edinburgh: T&T Clark, 1957.
———. *God Here and Now*. 2nd ed. London: Routledge, 2003.
Bauman, Zygmunt. *Liquid Love*. Boston: Polity, 2003.
Benedict XVI. "Homily of His Holiness Benedict XVI: Mass, Imposition of the Pallium and Conferral of the Fisherman's Ring for the Beginning of the Petrine Ministry of the Bishop of Rome." St. Peter's Square, Apr. 24, 2005. https://www.vatican.va/content/benedict-xvi/en/homilies/2005/documents/hf_ben-xvi_hom_20050424_inizio-pontificato.html.
Bixler, Sarah Ann. "A Great Co-Mission: Heeding Women's Problematization of 'Teaching Them.'" Presentation at Forum on Missional Hermeneutics, Society of Biblical Literature, Dec. 1, 2020.
Bosch, David. *Transforming Mission: Paradigm Shifts in Theology of Mission*. 20th anniversary ed. Maryknoll, NY: Orbis, 2011.
Burns, Bob, et al. *The Politics of Ministry: Navigating Power Dynamics and Negotiating Interests*. Downers Grove, IL: InterVarsity, 2019.
Byassee, Jason, Albert Y. S. Chu, and Ross A. Lockhart. *Christianity: An Asian Religion in Vancouver*. Eugene, OR: Cascade, 2023.

Calvin, John. *Institutes of the Christian Religion.* Louisville: Westminster/John Knox, 1960.

Cannon, Katie Geneva. "Christian Imperialism and the Transatlantic Slave Trade." *Journal of Feminist Studies in Religion* 24.1 (2008) 127–34.

Catechism of the Catholic Church. 2nd ed. Vatican City: Libreria Editrice Vaticana, 2011.

Cavanaugh, William T. *Being Consumed.* Grand Rapids: Eerdmans, 2008.

Chan, Michael J., and Brent A. Strawn. *What Kind of God? The Collected Essays of Terence E. Fretheim.* University Park, PA: Eisenbrauns, 2015.

Char, Meredith. *German American Partnership.* Colorado Springs: Nexus, 1991.

Chen, Ying, Eric S. Kim, and Tyler J. VanderWeele. "Religious-Service Attendance and Subsequent Health and Well-Being Throughout Adulthood: Evidence from Three Prospective Cohorts." *International Journal of Epidemiology* 49.6 (2020) 2030–40.

Coakley, Sarah. *God, Sexuality and the Self: An Essay on the Trinity.* Cambridge: Cambridge University Press, 2013.

"Defining Missional." *Leadership Journal* 29.4 (2008) 21.

Dickau, Tim. *Forming Christian Communities in a Secular Age.* Toronto: Tyndale Academic, 2021.

Dube, Musa W. *Postcolonial Feminist Interpretation of the Bible.* St. Louis: Chalice, 2000.

Dykxhoorn, J., et al. "Temporal Patterns in the Recorded Annual Incidence of Common Mental Disorders over Two Decades in the United Kingdom: A Primary Care Cohort Study." *Psychological Medicine* 54.4 (2024) 1–12.

Editors of Encyclopedia Britannica. "Hylomorphism." *Encyclopedia Britannica*, Mar. 15, 2016. https://www.britannica.com/topic/hylomorphism.

Editors of *Leadership Journal.* "Defining Missional." *Leadership Journal* 29.4 (2008) 20–22.

Ellis, Brendan. "4 Chestermere City Councillors, Including Mayor, Dismissed by Alberta Government Order." CTV News, Dec. 4, 2023. https://calgary.ctvnews.ca/4-chestermere-city-councillors-including-mayor-dismissed-by-alberta-government-order-1.6672982.

Ewell, Samuel E., III. *Faith Seeking Conviviality: Reflections on Ivan Illich, Christian Mission, and the Promise of Life Together.* Eugene, OR: Cascade, 2020.

Flett, John. *The Witness of God: The Trinity, Missio Dei, Karl Barth, and the Nature of the Christian Community.* Grand Rapids: Eerdmans, 2010.

Flett, John, and David Congdon, eds. *Converting Witness: The Future of Christian Mission in the New Millennium.* Lanham, MD: Lexington, 2019.

Guder, Darrell L. "Arguing Christianly: The Practice of Missional Unity in a Divisive Passage." Edwin H. Rian Alumni/ae Lectures, Princeton Theological Seminary, 2014. https://commons.ptsem.edu/id/8831.

———. *Be My Witnesses.* Grand Rapids: Eerdmans, 1985.

———. *Called to Witness: Doing Missional Theology.* Grand Rapids: Eerdmans, 2015.

———. "The Christians' Callings in the World: Pastoral Formation for Missional Vocation." *New Theology Review* 24.4 (2011) 6–16.

———. *The Continuing Conversion of the Church.* Grand Rapids: Eerdmans, 2000.

———. "Darrell Guder on Missional Communities." Fuller Seminary Archives, 2007 Payton Lectures, Dec. 4, 2020.

———. "Freeing Witness, Matthew 10." MP3. https://www.unionchurchseattle.org/sermons.

———. "From Mission and Theology to Missional Theology." *The Princeton Seminary Bulletin* 24.1 (2003) 36–54.

———. *The Incarnation and the Church's Witness*. Eugene, OR: Wipf & Stock, 1999.

———, ed. *Missional Church: A Vision for the Sending of the Church in North America*. Grand Rapids.: Eerdmans, 1998.

———. *Unlikely Ambassadors: Clay Jar Christians in God's Service*. Louisville: Presbyterian Publication Service, 2002.

———. "Walking Worthily: Missional Leadership After Christendom." *Princeton Theological Bulletin* 28.3 (2007) 251–91.

Hacker, Karen. "The Burden of Chronic Disease." *Mayo Clinic Proceedings: Innovations, Quality and Outcomes* 8.1 (2024) 112–19. https://www.mcpiqojournal.org/article/S2542-4548(23)00057-7/pdf.

The Halo Project. "The Halo Effect: Chestermere (AB)." Cardus, n.d. https://haloproject.ca/calculator/ab/chestermere.

Horgan, John. "Germ Theory." World History Encyclopedia, July 24, 2023. https://www.worldhistory.org/Germ_Theory/.

Hudson, Neil. *Imagine Church: Releasing Dynamic Everyday Disciples*. London: InterVarsity, 2012.

IFES. "Our Global Vision." https://ifesworld.org/en/vision/.

Jamieson, Bobby. *Understanding the Lord's Supper*. London: B&H, 2016.

Keller, Timothy. *Ministries of Mercy: The Call of the Jericho Road*. Phillipsburg, NJ: P&R, 2015.

Kierkegaard, Søren. *Purity of Heart Is to Will One Thing*. N.p.: Wilder, 2008.

Kreeft, Peter. *Practical Theology*. San Francisco: Ignatius, 2014.

Kreski, N. T., et al. "Explaining US Adolescent Depressive Symptom Trends Through Declines in Religious Beliefs and Service Attendance." *Journal of Religion and Health* 61 (2022) 300–326. https://doi.org/10.1007/s10943-021-01390-8.

Lockhart, Ross A., ed. *Christian Witness in Post-Christian Soil*. Eugene, OR: Cascade, 2021.

Luz, Ulrich. *Matthew: A Commentary*. Edited by Helmut Koester, translated by James E. Crouch. Hermeneia—A Critical and Historical Commentary on the Bible 3. Minneapolis: Fortress, 2005.

McCullough, Kate. "'We Are in Crisis Mode': Demand for School-Based Food Programs Soars in Hamilton." *Hamilton Spectator*, Dec. 22, 2022.

Newbigin, Lesslie. *Foolishness to the Greeks: The Gospel and Western Culture*. Grand Rapids: Eerdmans, 1986.

———. *The Gospel in a Pluralist Society*. Grand Rapids: Eerdmans, 1989.

———. *Mission in Christ's Way*. New York: Friendship, 1987.

———. "The Theory of Cross-Cultural Mission and the Ideology of Pluralism." 1984 Warfield Lectures, Princeton Theological Seminary. http://commons.ptsem.edu/id/04133#audio-player container.

Notkin, James B. "Ambassadors of Reconciliation." Sermon, Union Church Seattle, Dec. 2, 2007.

Ontario Agency for Health Protection and Promotion. "Household Food Insecurity Estimates from the Canadian Income Survey: Ontario 2019–2022." Toronto, ON: King's Printer for Ontario, 2023.

Peterson, Eugene. *The Jesus Way: A Conversation on the Ways That Jesus Is the Way*. Grand Rapids: Eerdmans, 2007.

Ratzinger, Joseph. "Concerning the Notion of Person in Theology." *Communio* 17 (1990).

———. *Introduction to Christianity*. Translated by J. R. Foster. San Francisco: Ignatius, 2004.
Reeves, Mike. "CU and the Church." The Christian Unions, n.d. https://www.uccf.org.uk/about/cu-and-church.
Rosa, Harmut. *The Uncontrollability of the World*. Boston: Polity, 2020.
Santomauro, Damian F., et al. "Global Prevalence and Burden of Depressive and Anxiety Disorders in 204 Countries and Territories in 2020 due to the COVID-19 Pandemic." *The Lancet* 398.10312 (2021) 1700–12. https://doi.org/10.1016/S0140-6736(21)02143-7.
Scherer, Sally. "Celebrating Darrell Guder, a Pioneer in Mission Theology." PC(USA), Nov. 27, 2020. https://pcusa.org/news-storytelling/news/2020/10/28/celebrating-darrell-guder-pioneer-mission-theology.
Segovia, Fernando F., and Mary Ann Tolbert, eds. *Teaching the Bible: The Discourses and Politics of Biblical Pedagogy*. Maryknoll, NY: Orbis, 1998.
Simon, D. H., and R. K. Masters. "Institutional Failures as Structural Determinants of Suicide: The Opioid Epidemic and the Great Recession in the United States." *Journal of Health and Social Behavior* 65.3 (2024) 415–31.
Sheen, Fulton J. *Peace of Soul*. New York: Whittlesey House, 1949.
Smith, Mitzi J., and Jayachitra Lalitha, eds. *Teaching All Nations: Interrogating the Matthean Great Commission*. Minneapolis: Fortress, 2014.
Stevens, Paul. *Liberating the Lady: Equipping All the Saints for Ministry*. Vancouver, BC: Regent College Publishing, 2002.
Stromberg, Jean, ed. *Mission and Evangelism: An Ecumenical Affirmation; A Study Guide for Congregations*. World Council of Churches, 1983. https://archive.org/details/wccmissionconfo50.
Substance Abuse and Mental Health Services Administration. *Key Substance Use and Mental Health Indicators in the United States: Results from the 2022 National Survey on Drug Use and Administration*. Center for Behavioral Health Statistics and Quality, Substance Abuse and Mental Health Services Administration, 2023. https://www.samhsa.gov/data/sites/default/files/reports/rpt42731/2022-nsduh-nnr.pdf.
Taylor, Charles. *A Secular Age*. Cambridge: Harvard University Press, 2007.
Thielicke, Helmut. *Notes from a Wayfarer: The Autobiography of Helmut Thielicke*. Translated by David Law. New York: Paragon, 1995.
UK Parliament. "Churchill and the Commons Chamber." N.d. https://www.parliament.uk/about/living-heritage/building/palace/architecture/palacestructure/churchill/.
VanderWeele, T. J., S. Li, and I. Kawachi. "Religious Service Attendance and Suicide Rates—Reply." *JAMA Psychiatry* 74.2 (2017) 197–98. doi:10.1001/jamapsychiatry.2016.2780.
Wilson, Jonathan R. *God's Good World: Reclaiming the Doctrine of Creation*. Grand Rapids: Baker Academic, 2013.
Winner, Lauren. *The Danger of Christian Practices*. New Haven: Yale University Press, 2018.
Winter, Ralph D. "The New Missions and the Mission of the Church." *International Review of Mission* 60.237 (1971) 89–100.

www.ingramcontent.com/pod-product-compliance
Lightning Source LLC
Chambersburg PA
CBHW021726220426
43662CB00008B/724